T0334642

Cambridge Elements ≡

Elements in New Religious Movements
Series Editor
Rebecca Moore
San Diego State University
Founding Editor
†James R. Lewis
Wuhan University

RELIGIOUS INNOVATION IN THE HELLENISTIC AND ROMAN PERIODS

Olav Hammer
University of Southern Denmark
Mikael Rothstein
University of Southern Denmark

CAMBRIDGE
UNIVERSITY PRESS

Shaftesbury Road, Cambridge CB2 8EA, United Kingdom

One Liberty Plaza, 20th Floor, New York, NY 10006, USA

477 Williamstown Road, Port Melbourne, VIC 3207, Australia

314–321, 3rd Floor, Plot 3, Splendor Forum, Jasola District Centre, New Delhi – 110025, India

103 Penang Road, #05–06/07, Visioncrest Commercial, Singapore 238467

Cambridge University Press is part of Cambridge University Press & Assessment, a department of the University of Cambridge.

We share the University's mission to contribute to society through the pursuit of education, learning and research at the highest international levels of excellence.

www.cambridge.org
Information on this title: www.cambridge.org/9781009015257

DOI: 10.1017/9781009030106

First published 2023

A catalogue record for this publication is available from the British Library.

ISBN 978-1-009-01525-7 Paperback
ISSN 2635-232X (online)
ISSN 2635-2311 (print)

Religious Innovation in the Hellenistic and Roman Periods

Elements in New Religious Movements

DOI: 10.1017/9781009030106
First published online: July 2023

Olav Hammer
University of Southern Denmark

Mikael Rothstein
University of Southern Denmark

Author for correspondence: Olav Hammer, ohammer@sdu.dk

Abstract: The scholarly study of new religious movements focuses on the contemporary period, but religious innovation is nothing new. This Element explores two historical epochs characterized by a multitude of emergent religious concepts and practices – the Hellenistic and Roman periods. A precondition for the intense degree of religious innovation during this time was a high level of cultural exchange. Religious elements crossed porous cultural borders and were adapted to suit new purposes. The resulting amalgams were presented in a vast corpus of texts, largely produced by a literate elite. Charismatic leaders played a particularly important role in creating new religious options and were described in genres infused with ideological agendas. Novel religious developments were accepted by the Roman authorities unless suspected of undermining the social order. The rise of one of the many new religions of the period, Christianity, ultimately changed the religious landscape in profound ways.

Keywords: Hellenistic and Roman periods, religious innovation, new religions, religious texts, charisma, religious conflict, religious polemics

ISBNs: 9781009015257 (PB), 9781009030106 (OC)
ISSNs: 2635-232X (online), 2635-2311 (print)

Contents

Introduction

The Hellenistic and Roman periods were characterized by a high degree of religious pluralism and innovation. Then as now, new religious phenomena tended in fact to not be completely original. Much of the mosaic of religious practices in the Hellenistic and Roman periods – the era of roughly seven centuries from the time of Alexander the Great (356–323 BCE) to the imposition by law of Christianity as the sole religion of the Roman Empire at the end of the fourth century CE – retained the focus on life here and now that also typified many older forms of Greek and Roman religion. Ideas that had older roots but now gained particular prominence included the notion that the soul is held prisoner in the body, and that deities exist who can help people navigate the chaos of a capricious destiny and provide them with a better afterlife.

Many innovations were the result of encounters with the religious concepts and practices of peoples with whom the Greeks and Romans interacted in what we might call a regionally globalized world. When they were adopted by Greeks and Romans, such imports were reinterpreted to fit the preconceptions and interests of their recipients. Section 1 of our Element explores some of the ways in which religious concepts, myths, rituals, and objects could be borrowed and adapted.

Although such sources as objects and images also provide important insights into religious life in antiquity, much of our knowledge about religion and religious innovations in the period under consideration is due to the fact that writers produced a wealth of texts documenting myths about the gods, speculation about life after death, records of days when communal rituals should be performed, methods that could be used to influence others by magical means, polemics against other religions, and much else besides. One of the innovations of the period that would prove to have a particularly long-lasting influence was the emergence of a sacrosanct subset of religious writings – that is, canons by which members of a religious community defined their collective identity. Section 2 presents some of the textual genres of the period and introduces a number of key characteristics of canonical texts.

Most religious innovations are local, are short-lived, and have a very limited impact on society. This is true today, and it was true during the periods in focus here. When they did leave their mark on history, a charismatic leader, a holy man or woman, or some other kind of religious entrepreneur was often instrumental in the process. Like founders of innovative religions in our own time, such individuals are often portrayed as superhuman. Section 3 is devoted to presenting five such figures, highlighting both what is known of their historical role as religious innovators and the characteristic features of the textual genres that describe them.

The chronological end point of our Element is the late fourth century CE, a time marked by the imposition by law of Christianity in the Roman Empire. Although the attempt to enforce a single ideology profoundly changed what had previously been a heterogeneous religious landscape, boundaries in the preceding Hellenistic and Roman periods were also drawn between what people considered acceptable and unacceptable religion. Focusing on the Roman period, we will in Section 4 briefly present some of the ways in which such boundary work was carried out against undesirable religious phenomena.

1 A World of Regional Globalization

It may seem counterintuitive to begin a survey of religious innovation in Hellenistic and Roman times by introducing a concept that has become emblematic of our own age, namely globalization. This term, in short, denotes a process of integration where goods, money, ideas, languages, and people transcend geographical barriers, allowing new cultural structures to develop. The rate and scope of the phenomenon has increased with the introduction of improved or novel means of long-distance transportation and modern means of communication, not least the Internet. The current level of interconnectedness is unlike anything humankind has previously experienced, and it has for decades been commonplace to talk of the entire world as "a single place" (Robertson 1991: 283). In antiquity, the degree and scale of contact across ethnic, cultural, and geographical divides was, of course, more restricted. Nevertheless, material goods, people, and cultural elements did flow over considerable distances in what we will call regional globalization. Although we need to proceed cautiously when comparing two periods separated by such a vast span of time, the similarities between the religious landscapes then and now are striking, and there is no doubt that many religious innovations were due not least to the transmission of religious elements across ethnic and cultural borders. In the process, new meanings for concepts and practices were negotiated, innovative ideas and practices emerged, and new religions came into being.

The beginning of the Hellenistic period is often perceived as a time of intensified cultural exchange, but no group lives in isolation, and such elements of a religious tradition as myths can reveal far more ancient patterns of religious regional globalization. The striking parallels between Hesiod's *Theogony* (composed around 700 BCE) and various creation myths of the ancient Near East, for instance, have been extensively examined (Kelly and Metcalfe 2021). The similarities between biblical myths and older Near Eastern narratives provide another example. The arguably best-known example is the ways in which Mesopotamian myths relating how the gods decided to eradicate humanity by inundating the world and how a small group of people survived in a boat are echoed in the biblical flood narrative (Dalley 2000). Hence, the regional globalization of Hellenistic and Roman times was not a completely novel phenomenon but a striking escalation of already existing processes.

This accelerated interchange was a consequence of military expansions in the late fourth century BCE. Macedonia, once a minor kingdom on the periphery of the Greek world, had during the reign of Philip II (382–336 BCE) extended its power and had come to dominate Greece and the southern Balkans. After these victories, the Macedonian armies turned eastward, but Philip was assassinated and further conquests were left to his son, Alexander. In 334 BCE, Alexander set in motion a military campaign that lasted for eleven years and turned out to be so successful that he would become known as "the Great." After crossing the Dardanelles in the spring of that year, his army proceeded to conquer vast territories in Asia Minor, the eastern coastal Mediterranean region, Egypt, Mesopotamia, and Persia, and Alexander led his troops as far as to present-day Pakistan and northern India. Upon his death in 323 BCE, this vast territory soon fell apart and was divided, after a series of wars, between his commanders. The resulting kingdoms attracted Greek colonists, Greek became the language of the elite, and Greek and local customs cross-fertilized (Worthington 2014). Trade and migration also led to the rise of major, multicultural cities such as Alexandria, Pergamon, Antioch, and, later, Rome, many of whose residents had roots elsewhere. As a consequence, religious traditions were often practiced in settings detached from their previous contexts, and in order to remain meaningful and functional, they had to be adapted or even radically refashioned (Podemann Sørensen 2011: 146). Although our focus is squarely on the dissemination of cultural elements and their innovative interpretations and uses, we should bear in mind that the Hellenistic and Roman period also saw its share of attempts to preserve religious traditions under conditions of massive social change and of religious innovations taking place within a community for other reasons than as a response to regional globalization.[1]

Religious Interaction and Syncretism

The Hellenistic and Roman religious landscape did not consist of bounded entities, separate religions, that were practiced according to officially sanctioned and set ways. Rather, what we for ease of reference can call religion or religions was a mosaic of flexible ideas about the deities and how one can interact with them. In the Roman period, a pantheon of gods known to many people throughout the empire (Jupiter, Mars, etc.) coexisted with a vast array of

---

[1] See Podemann Sørensen 1989 and Weinholt 1989 for discussions of such processes.

other superhuman beings – for instance, local deities or lesser divinities that were assumed to intervene in human life. Since the superhuman realm was fluid and the range of ritual activities directed at these beings was open-ended, religious practices and concepts could also be borrowed from people outside the Greek and Roman cultural spheres.

Then as now, foreign imports need to make sense within their new cultural context. Contemporary examples abound. Yoga can be pursued for reasons such as health and well-being that have no connection with the soteriological aims of yoga in a classical Indian context. Modern religious practices loosely modeled on indigenous shamanic traditions, and hence often referred to as neoshamanism, are widespread in New Age milieus among people who have no intention of adopting the specific practices of shamans in a particular ethnic setting. The introduction of foreign religious elements into a Greek or Roman context involved similar processes of sometimes quite radical reinterpretation. A key feature of Greek and Roman religions that facilitated such processes of religious interaction was *interpretatio graeca* and its later counterpart, *interpretatio romana* – the ready identification of foreign deities with one's own gods based on the assumption that if they served similar functions, they could be considered in some sense "the same gods" albeit with different names. Being "the same," gods that had foreign roots could be worshipped in ways familiar to Greeks or Romans.

One result of this process of interpretation and translation are references to deities identified by a string of several names, Greek as well as foreign. Jenny Wallensten (2014) has examined a number of such composite gods. Greek votive inscriptions from the island of Delos refer to "Astarte Palaistine Aphrodite Ourania" and "Isis Soteira Astarte Aphrodite Euploia Epekoos," the latter apparently worshipped in conjunction with "Eros Harpokrates Apollon," while the doubly named Isis Aphrodite is attested from a wider area. Deities such as these, often referred to in the scholarly literature as being syncretistic, are, according to Wallensten, better seen as the products of individuals who lived in a multicultural reality and who deliberately drew upon (in this particular case) their Phoenician and Greek cultural competence in order to translate between religious traditions and convey to human and divine audiences precisely to whom their inscription was dedicated. Taking this specific work of intercultural translation as symptomatic of its times, Hellenistic globalization (and, later, its Roman counterpart) comes across first and foremost as a way of perceiving the world, perhaps not as a single place, but as a place where boundaries were porous, familiarity with religious Others was common, and the exchange between cultures was normal.

Deities of foreign origin were imported across such porous boundaries and assimilated to what was already familiar by a remarkable variety of historically contingent processes. The veneration of some of these imported and adapted gods became major elements of the religious landscape. A few examples can illustrate the diversity of pathways of amalgamation. Our first case is the development in Hellenistic and Roman worlds of the cult of Isis. In her original Egyptian setting, she played numerous roles.[2] An elaborate myth presented her as the consort of Osiris, whom she brought back to life after the evil Seth had killed him. With her revived husband, she then conceived a son, Horus. This drama of the triumph of good over evil became a mythological charter for the pharaoh's role as guarantor of order, and by the middle of the last millennium BCE, Isis had become one of the most important deities of the Egyptian pantheon. Shortly before 300 BCE, the cult of Isis reached Greece, and soon she became a popular deity there also.

In Egyptian religion, Isis had by then become associated with the goddess of grain, which in the new context led her to be assimilated to the corresponding Greek goddess, Demeter. One of the social settings of Greek and, later, Roman religion were mystery cults – that is, voluntary associations of people who had been initiated into a community dedicated to the worship of a specific deity. The prototypical example of a mystery cult was the Eleusinian mysteries, devoted to Demeter. Through association, Isis also became the central character of an initiatory cult that probably had no counterpart in the goddess's Egyptian homeland. Isis had now become the ally of the initiate, the protector and savior of the individual who would ask for her blessings. From Greece, the Isis mysteries came to the Italian peninsula, reaching Rome in the first century BCE. Over the centuries, Isis accumulated an ever-broader variety of divine functions and attributes, ultimately transforming her into a deity of universal scope who could confer good fortune upon her devotees. Her universality comes across in a passage in a novel by the Roman author Apuleius (ca. 120–ca. 170 CE), *Metamorphoses* (11, 5; also known as *The Golden Ass*), in which Isis is presented as identical to a range of other deities, a list Luther Martin (1983) argues is based upon a perception of systematic resemblances between these figures. Isis proclaims how she is revered under countless names throughout "the entire world" – that is, the globalized region that the author was aware of:

> [T]he entire world worships my single godhead in a thousand shapes, with diverse rites, and under many a different name. The Phrygians, first-born of mankind, call me the Pessinuntian Mother of the gods; the native Athenians

---

[2] On the role of Isis in Egypt, see Münster 1968. Our description of the cult's Hellenization is a summary of Bøgh 2013.

the Cecropian Minerva; the island-dwelling Cypriots Paphian Venus; the archer Cretans Dictynnan Diana; the triple-tongued Sicilians Stygian Proserpine; the ancient Eleusinians Actaean Ceres; some call me Juno, some Bellona, others Hecate, others Rhamnusia; but both races of Ethiopians, those on whom the rising and those on whom the setting sun shines, and the Egyptians who excel in ancient learning, honour me with the worship which is truly mine and call me by my true name: Queen Isis. (Apuleius, *Metamorphoses* XI, 5)[3]

Our next case concerns a goddess from Asia Minor who was brought to Greece and Rome, where she was adapted to local religious conceptions: Cybele.[4] The veneration of a mother deity associated with mountains had a long local history in Phrygia, in what is today a region in western Turkey. By the sixth century BCE, the goddess had been adopted in Greece and numerous shrines to her were erected. Her popularity increased in the Hellenistic period, and in 205 BCE, the cult took the leap from the Hellenized coast of Asia Minor to Rome. In his *History of Rome* (29, 10–14), the Roman historian Livy (59 BCE–17 CE) relates how, during the Second Punic War (218–201 BCE), a shower of stones was interpreted as an omen that foretold the doom of the Republic. The Sibylline oracle was consulted, and a prophecy revealed that Rome would prevail if the Mother Goddess was brought to the city. Whatever the historical facts behind the traditional account may have been, the new deity from faraway Phrygia was in 191 BCE installed in a temple on the Palatine, in the shape of a black meteoric rock.[5] The cult of Cybele was overseen by castrated Phrygian priests, *galli*, whose flamboyant dress and ecstatic rituals were deeply foreign to Roman customs. The trust of the Romans in the oracle, however, was deeply rooted, and it was so imperative to follow its injunctions that the presence of the goddess in Rome was accepted and festivals were held in her honor. By imperial times, the cult had spread over large parts of the Roman Empire, and Cybele had somewhat paradoxically morphed from a local Phrygian deity to both a deity of the state and hence a major fixture of the Roman religious landscape and a cult that continued to be associated with the detested *galli*.

We know far less about another amalgamated deity, Jupiter Dolichenus, since material evidence such as archaeological findings needs to be interpreted with the aid of few and rather uninformative written sources.[6] This was a god from

---

[3] All primary sources quoted in the text are listed separately in the references, before the secondary literature.

[4] The information given here is based on Roller 1999. We will return to the cult of Cybele in greater detail in Section 4.

[5] See Gruen 1992 and Burton 1996 for varying opinions.

[6] On Jupiter Dolichenus, see Beard, North, and Price 1998: 275, Blömer and Winter 2012, and Vitas 2021: 92–113.

the city of Doliche in northern Syria – an area that, due to shifting borders, is today southeastern Turkey. When imported into Rome, he was transformed into the god of a mystery religion. The globalizing process involved in the creation of the deity and his cult is revealed already in the name of the divinity, since this was originally the Syrian god Ba'al. The characteristic iconography of Jupiter Dolichenus also speaks of a thorough Romanization of the god: he is represented as a bearded man wearing a Phrygian cap but otherwise dressed in Roman attire, who stands on the back of a bull holding a double-headed axe and a thunderbolt. His followers, many of whom were soldiers and traders, were organized according to the same basic principles as devotees of other mystery cults – that is, as a hierarchy distinguished by various levels of initiation. Furthermore, the cult of Jupiter Dolichenus was also very popular among people without Syrian roots. The rapid spread of the cult even to such peripheries of the Roman Empire as Britain and the Rhine area, presumably by following military networks of communication, is an indication of how efficient regional globalization could be, and of the wandering cult's ability to find a home in new places. Exchange across boundaries is also apparent from the array of deities present in his sanctuary on the Aventine in Rome – besides Jupiter Dolichenus himself, there were effigies of the Greco-Roman gods Diana, Hercules, and Apollo and of foreign imports such as Mithras and various Egyptian deities (Beard, North, and Price 1998: 281).

A major attraction of participating in such elective cults would have been the benefits, in this life and in the next, that ensued from dedication to a powerful and caring deity.[7] The sheer fact that these gods and their rituals had exotic origins may have contributed to their authority and appeal, although we will see in Section 4 that the foreignness of the deities could also cause conflicts and controversies. Texts that describe these cults reflect the perspective of a literate elite, but there is evidence that exoticism could have a wider appeal. After the incorporation of Egypt into the Roman Empire in 31 BCE, interest in all things Egyptian exploded, and Isis was increasingly celebrated in Egyptian – or at least imagined Egyptian – style.

In some cases, the exotic – that is, references to foreign religious conceptions and imports of foreign deities – could serve a deliberate political aim. An oracle in a temple in the oasis of Siwa in the borderland between Egypt and Libya was connected with the god Amon-Re, and the Greeks had a well-established tradition, documented already in Herodotus's *Histories* written in the fifth century BCE, of seeing this deity as identical to their own Zeus. The concept of the ruler's divine parentage had deep roots in Egyptian religion but was seen

---

[7] For a discussion of the appeal of these cults, see Beard, North, and Price 1998: 278–91.

as foreign in the Greek cultural sphere; yet when Alexander visited the oracle, the sources tell us, he was informed by the deity that he was the son of the presiding god.[8] After Alexander's death, the vast area he had conquered fragmented, a war of succession broke out, and in 305/304, Ptolemy I (ca. 367–283 BCE) emerged as the ruler of Egypt and the founder of a new dynasty. His attempt to achieve legitimacy as a Hellenic ruler of a Greek elite and a large Egyptian population involved a process of religious amalgamation that involved creating a new cult with echoes of both cultures. Originally an Egyptian composite deity, Osiris-Apis combined the name of the patron deity of the pharaoh, Osiris, with that of the bull deity Apis, venerated in the city of Memphis and represented by embalmed bulls that were worshipped in their tombs. Following a common trope that gave divine authority to a religious innovation, Ptolemy I related a dream in which he was told to bring the statue of a hitherto unknown god to the recently founded city of Alexandria (Plutarch, *On Isis and Osiris*, 361 f–362 c). When the new god, now Hellenized as Serapis, was introduced, he was not represented in any traditional Egyptian form but had an entirely anthropomorphic appearance, namely as a man with a beard, not unlike the depictions of well-known Greek gods. Soon, Serapis became associated with Isis, an obvious echo of the divine sibling-couple of Osiris and Isis that had been the dynastic deities of the pharaohs. The Egyptian-style divinization of the rulers also became a core element of Ptolemaic rule, and as monarchs succeeded each other, living and deceased god-kings and their goddess consorts were added to the cult. The interplay of Hellenistic syncretism and personal innovation that characterized various stages of the dynastic cult can be judged from the fact that around 116 BCE, Cleopatra III became the object of rituals that associated the queen with the Greek goddess Demeter and required the services of three priestesses and two priests.[9]

The Spread of Christianity

A continuous and almost open-ended religious exchange may have been the norm in the Hellenistic and Roman religious landscape, but the most successful new religion that arose in the epoch we cover in this Element was characterized by its rejection of that norm and its denunciation of all other religions as false. We will return to the controversies and conflicts that resulted from this core belief in Section 4. Here, we will present what the limited available data say

---

[8] For a summary of the events with references to sources and previous scholarship, see Collins 2014.

[9] On Serapis and the Ptolemaic dynastic cult, see Dunand 2007: 259–62.

about the rate of growth of Christianity and summarize what scholars have identified as plausible reasons for its success.

Over the centuries, Christianity gathered an unprecedented number of adherents.[10] How quick this expansion was and how it was achieved remains a point of debate. At one end of the spectrum of possibilities, Christians were still a small minority by the time Emperor Theodosius decided to legally impose a particular version of Christianity. Drawing upon archaeological evidence, Ramsay MacMullen (2009: 112–13) suggests that they still constituted only 3 percent of the population and that any assessment of their growth in the centuries that followed remains "guesswork." The eventual success of Christianity, on this account, was due largely to the fact that an elite with political and economic power gradually managed to impose the new religion. At the other end of the spectrum, it has often been asserted that Christians, after a modest start, had by the cusp of the fourth century grown to vast numbers and had spread rapidly over great distances. An early attempt to assess the size of the Christian community and their rate of growth in late antiquity by means of demographic models and statistics was made by sociologist of religion Rodney Stark in his book *The Rise of Christianity* (1996: 6–13). Several scholars have since then revised the figures he arrived at – for example, Bart Ehrman (2018), whose figures we quote here. They were a diminutive group at the time of Jesus's death, perhaps a mere twenty people. Thirty years later, around the year 60 CE, there were probably still only approximately 1,000 to 1,500. The sheer fact that growth was exponential, however, meant that by the year 200 CE, their number may have grown to somewhere in the range between 140,000 and 170,000 people. According to the same model of exponential growth, the curve would have continued to climb, and by the time pagan Roman culture approached its final days and Christianity took over as the hegemonic religion of the Empire near the cusp of the fifth century, there may, as per Ehrman's assessment, have been 30 million Christians.

Whether it took three centuries or longer to grow to such numbers, Christianity over time reached far beyond the confines of the Roman Empire and thus transcended the regional globalization that was characteristic of antiquity, eventually becoming a global phenomenon also in the full sense of the term. Religious insiders may be tempted to attribute the remarkable success of the new religion to

---

[10] Although we will on occasion collectively refer to the groups of Jesus-centered devotees in the first centuries following the death of Jesus as Christians and their beliefs and practices as Christianity, it should be noted that this is a stylistic choice adopted in order to avoid repeatedly using lengthy but more precise labels. Followers of Jesus venerated him in countless diverse ways, and the degree to which they perceived of themselves as separate from the Jewish community varied.

its supposedly unique (and by implication superior) teachings. Much of early Christianity would, however, have been quite recognizable within its cultural context. Christianity was structurally similar to the mystery religions of antiquity. These religions consisted of communities of people united by devotion to a particular deity and ritually initiated into that fellowship. In more this-worldly terms, the community of Christians offered a sense of belonging and an extended social service network, but so did other initiatory organizations. The Christian deity offered comfort and salvation to individuals who joined his community, as did the gods of other religions centered on devotion to a particular deity. The claim that Jesus was both divine and human reflected a conceptualization of divinity that was common in the first centuries CE (Ehrman 2014). Jesus was immediately accessible during rituals and devotees could have a very emotional and intimate relationship with him, just as members of other mysteries could have with the deities they worshipped. Initiates revered a god who had died and returned to life, a theme with many variations that Christianity shared with other religions (Mettinger 2001). The details vary from one deity-centered movement to another, but the fact that the Jesus movement struck roughly the same balance as others between continuity and change and, like them, combined well-known religious perspectives and new ideas, requires us to look elsewhere for the features that gave precisely this movement its competitive edge over all others. Scholars have identified several such key factors.

First, Christianity was open to new members irrespective of their social status, gender, age, or ethnic background. Universality also entailed that when the convert was the head of a family, the patriarchal norms of the time could lead all other members of the family to also became Christians. Second, gods in the fluid world of Roman religion were understood to be powerful beings and were expected to bestow benefits upon those who honored them. The new Jesus-centered religion lived up to these expectations: sources that describe conversions relate how people became convinced that important figures in the Christian community were able to effect miracles. Whether they directly witnessed events that they understood to be miraculous or gave credence to stories narrated by others, they became assured of the power of the Christian god and converted. Third, Christianity differed from other religious currents in its insistence on possessing an exclusive truth. People who converted to Christianity would not necessarily adopt a set of practices or concepts that aligned with the views of the religious elite. Nonetheless, efforts to draw boundaries and ensure that orthodoxy was upheld were part and parcel of the new religion. By contrast, those who joined communities devoted to other gods were not expected to withdraw from participating in whatever other practices in which they were already involved.

A comparison between the ritual venerations of Mithras and Jesus shows the stark difference between them in these respects. Military personnel, civil servants, and merchants constituted the bulk of members of the cult of Mithras, and presumably the benefits this god could bestow were especially attractive to men in these categories. The cult was certainly not universal, and women were in fact barred from joining. Mithras did not compete with other gods: those who felt attracted to the cult of Mithras and were initiated into this particular religious option could continue to participate in any number of other religious activities. It is not even clear how a concept like conversion would apply to a practice that functioned as an add-on to an open set of other practices one could keep on pursuing. Mithraism was by its very nature therefore hardly in a position to become a dominant religion that ousted others. William Van Andringa notes that:

> The growing success of the cult of Mithras at this time had nothing to do with any public impulse in Rome or the cities, but rather fell within the framework of a broadening of religious options typical of polytheism . . . the cult openly implanted itself in the religious district of the civic group, city or *vicus*, without entering into competition with the traditional religion, which continued to be largely dominated by the great communal cults. (Andringa 2007: 90)

The Christian claim that there is only one true religion and only one god who may be worshipped went hand in hand with another teaching that distinguished it from other mystery cults, namely the insistence that nonbelievers would meet a horrible fate. Mystery religions in general were predicated on the belief that initiates were qualitatively different from the mass of the uninitiated. A fragment by Plutarch (45–120 CE), for instance, explains how a person who is initiated "surveys the uninitiated, unpurified mob here on earth, the mob of living men who, herded together in mirk and deep mire, trample one another down and in their fear of death cling to their ills, since they disbelieve in the blessings of the other world" (Plutarch, *Moralia*, Vol. XV, fragment 178).[11] The Christians, however, took the distinction between initiated insiders and those left outside the boundary to new levels. Early sources state that those who are not part of the community are destined to annihilation. According to the Second Epistle to the Thessalonians (a text from the middle of the first century CE, traditionally attributed to Paul but of disputed authorship), in a not-too-far eschatological future:

> Lord Jesus is revealed from heaven with his mighty angels in flaming fire, inflicting vengeance on those who do not know God and on those who do not

---

[11] The quote is an excerpt, reproduced in a fifth-century anthology generally referred to as the Stobaeus, from an otherwise lost work by Plutarch.

obey the gospel of our Lord Jesus. These will suffer the punishment of eternal destruction, separated from the presence of the Lord and from the glory of his might, when he comes to be glorified by his saints and to be marveled at on that day among all who have believed, because our testimony to you was believed. (2 Thessalonians 1:7–10)

Beginning in the second century CE, new and potentially even more horrendous prospects were presented as the fate of those who fall on the wrong side of the boundary. Rather than being obliterated, they face an eternity of unimaginable suffering. The earliest source describing these torments is the *Apocalypse of Peter*, probably composed in the first half of that century. Sinners, including those who place themselves outside the Christian fold, are tortured in inventive ways that match the nature of their sins. Those who "forsook the way of God" are roasted in a pan, while those who "blaspheme and speak evil of the way of righteousness" have their eyes burned with hot irons.[12] The success of Christianity, Ehrman quite plausibly suggests, was not least due to the sheer terror it could instill in potential converts (Ehrman 2018: 153–4). Presumably, the same terror could also prompt people who had become Christians to remain committed to their new religion.

2 Religious Texts

There are at first glance rather obvious differences between how information about religious matters circulated in antiquity and in the modern world. We live in a mediatized and globalized world. We have at our disposal innumerable texts, films, video clips, websites, and other media that document – or at least purport to document – religious traditions from around the globe. The Hellenistic and Roman worlds, of course, were characterized by a very different level of technology and were regionally rather than globally connected. Besides being reproduced through the spoken word, information about religion was disseminated via texts laboriously copied by hand. The immediate impact of such texts was limited by low rates of literacy. These rates are hard to assess, but an estimate by a leading scholar on the period is that perhaps 20 percent or fewer of men could read, whereas women were illiterate to an even greater extent (Beard 2004: 128–9). Access to texts on religious topics was hence restricted to a cultural elite. Most people would have encountered religion by participating in rituals, visiting religious sites, and listening to religious topics being spoken about.

---

[12] *Apocalypse of Peter*, verses 28 (blasphemers) and 34 (forsaking the way of God).

Despite such strictures, writers in antiquity produced a wealth of documents about the gods, life after death, oracles and omens, the correct dates on which to carry out communal rituals, the steps necessary to influence others by magical means, and many other topics. We shall return to illustrative examples of such texts. In his seminal book, *Orality and Literacy*, Walter J. Ong argued in 1982 that the transition to a culture of writing had far-reaching consequences. In an oral culture, all that can be known is what somebody can recall. The very existence of written materials enabled forms of cultural memory to arise that preliterate societies could not muster. Once there was such an external memory store that recorded doctrines, myths, or ritual practices, they became part of the cultural landscape and could be consulted and commented upon by others. Unless every copy was destroyed or removed from public access, even texts that had passed into oblivion could later be retrieved from obscurity and become the focus of renewed interest and exegetical efforts.

Judaism and Christianity gave written texts a particularly central role.[13] Out of the mass of written materials, a core of writings came to be selected as a canon. The concept of a sacrosanct subset of texts spread to later religions, such as Manichaeism and Islam, and over time became a ubiquitous feature of emergent religions. Innumerable new religious movements in our own time have a set of key texts that authoritatively stipulate which doctrinal statements are valid or dictate the correct performance of rituals. Authority in such movements lies with the text itself and with the person who has the authority to interpret it.

Most religions in antiquity were not in the same way centered around a sacrosanct canon, and, more generally, few religious currents from that time are presented in the form of systematic compilations of doctrinal statements and theological elaborations of concepts and narratives recorded in texts. Much of religious life was based on the performance of ritual acts rather than on the profession of belief in particular doctrines. We consequently have a fair amount of evidence of what people did and how religious life was organized, but few explanations of what it all meant. An illustrative example is Mithraism, a religion that was widespread in the Roman Empire from perhaps the first century of the Common Era – although the historical beginnings of Mithraism in Rome remain disputed. The copious sources include votive inscriptions, reliefs, underground chambers where rituals were carried out, and various other archaeological remains. These sources document a religion that in particular attracted members outside the highest echelons of Roman society, soldiers and minor officials in particular, in which members were organized in an

---

[13] Beard 2004 provides a nuanced discussion of the issues involved.

initiatory hierarchy, and where a central complex of myths and rituals concerned the slaying of a bull by the god Mithras. What the narrative about the deity consisted of, however, is far from clear to modern researchers. Few written sources provide any information, and it is not obvious how the archaeological evidence is to be pieced together and understood.[14]

The sources we do have can be frustratingly vague. One reason for this is that the authors of texts in antiquity addressed readers who belonged to the same cultural context and did not need the details spelled out. The dearth of written sources documenting what we might think of as the core elements of various religions is in part also accounted for by the fact that some religions in antiquity imposed varying degrees of secrecy. Texts that break the silence and describe such religious phenomena can be circumspect. For instance, in Book XI of Apuleius's *Metamorphoses*, the reader is presented with the story of the narrator's initiation into the cult of Isis. The book relates the fate of a young man, Lucius, who is by accident magically transformed into a donkey. After Lucius undergoes numerous rather unpleasant adventures, Isis turns him back into human form and he pledges to be initiated. Apuleius, who may have been an initiate himself, describes the ritual:

> I dare say, attentive reader, that you are all agog to know what was then said and done. I should tell you if it were lawful to tell it; you should learn if it were lawful to hear it. But then your ears and my tongue would both incur equal guilt, the one for sacrilegious loquacity, the other for importunate curiosity. But since it may be that your anxious yearning is piously motivated, I will not torment you by prolonging your anguish. Listen then, but believe; for what I tell you is the truth. I came to the boundary of death and after treading Proserpine's threshold I returned having traversed all the elements; at midnight I saw the sun shining with brilliant light; I approached the gods below and the gods above face to face and worshipped them in their actual presence. Now I have told you what, though you have heard it, you cannot know. So all that can without sin be revealed to the understanding of the uninitiated, that and no more I shall relate. (Apuleius, *Metamorphoses* XI, 23)

Despite the author's insistence that it is not lawful for him to reveal much of the initiation, sources at our disposal provide clues. A textual genre that sheds light on the drama is the aretalogy, a set of self-congratulatory proclamations attributed to various gods, particularly those of foreign origin. Such first-person narratives were known from inscriptions on temples and statues, but also from literature, and typically referred to the great deeds and qualities myths and legends reported about these deities and that made them worthy of veneration. Aretalogies may have served as hymns or liturgies during rituals, but we

---

[14] For a succinct introduction to the interpretive challenges, see Clauss 2013.

may also understand them as theological doctrines expounding the nature and will of the divinity. The Isis aretalogy of Kyme (dating from the first century BCE or first century CE) is an elaborate example comprised of some sixty verses. The text has been analyzed as a combination of Egyptian tropes that present Isis as an all-powerful, cosmic deity and Hellenistic-Roman concepts of her as a loving and caring guardian of those who seek her protection (Bergman 1968).

Upon his departure from the temple where his initiation took place, Lucius gives thanks to Isis. Kneeling before the cult statue, weeping from joy, he says (Apuleius, *Metamorphoses* XI, 25): "Hail, holy one, eternal saviour of the human race, ever cherishing mortals with your bounty, you who extend a mother's tender love to the sufferings of the unfortunate" – and the praise goes on and on. Lucius's words reflect elements of the aretalogy, couched in a literary representation of what initiates such as Lucius and his peers felt as a result of their initiation.

Plausible examples of the putative Egyptian connection of the ritual include the notion of the sun passing through the underworld and the idea of the dead traversing the entire cosmos and being in the immediate presence of the gods. In the context of a mystery cult, this combination of motifs is used to lead the neophyte to a new life beyond a symbolic death, whereas in ancient Egypt, it was a reference to the regenerative power of the sun and of nature (Podemann Sørensen 2011). Isis and the religious notions relating to her had thus been profoundly reconfigured over the span of many centuries and in the transition to new cultural contexts, and these changes are evidenced in the sources at our disposal.

The interpretation of the initiation ritual we have just sketched reflects the fact that the Isis cult did not have a literati elite who elaborated a corpus of theological statements and developed a commentarial tradition. As we have seen, our understanding of the events needs to be pieced together from the narratives we do have and from a cautious identification of similarities with Egyptian conceptions of Isis. The picture arrived at may be plausible and supported by evidence, but the interpretive challenges are of a different order than those facing readers of the elaborate theological statements produced within religious traditions where the written word is paramount.

The complex relationship between textual evidence and lived religion is illustrated by another initiatory tradition, the Eleusinian mysteries. The oldest of the various mystery religions, the Eleusinian mysteries had origins that far predate the Hellenistic and Roman periods considered here, but they continued to be practiced until their demise in the late fourth century CE. They involved rituals performed in the open for all to witness and a secret initiation that authors of antiquity only cautiously alluded to. The public parts of this collective festival are recorded in some detail, and it is clear that the myth of the goddess Demeter and her daughter Persephone was closely connected to the ritual activities. According to the most elaborate version of this myth, as recorded in the so-called *Homeric Hymn to Demeter*, Persephone was abducted by the god of the underworld, Hades. Demeter, distraught at the news, adopted human shape and set out on a journey that led her to Eleusis, a town located some 20 kilometers (12 miles) from Athens. Keleos, the king of Eleusis, invited her to join the royal household as a nurse to his infant son, Demophon, and Demeter set out to transform the child into a deity by placing him in the fire every night. One night, Demophon's mother happened to see this alarming scene and became understandably upset at what was unfolding before her eyes. Demeter revealed her true identity, proclaimed the young boy would henceforth be mortal like all other humans, and commanded the locals to build a temple and to carry out a series of rites that she divulged to them.

The etiological nature of the *Homeric Hymn to Demeter* seems evident: rituals are to be performed, and the setting of these rituals is where the central events of the myth take place. Furthermore, several details in the ritual correspond to events recounted in the *Hymn to Demeter* – for instance, the goddess is given a beverage called *kykeon* consisting of barley and pennyroyal, a drink the participants in the ritual also consume. Just as clearly, however, the hymn is not a straightforward guide to the ritual events. Kevin Clinton, a leading authority on the Eleusinian mysteries, concludes on the basis of a close comparison of the text with iconographic evidence and other sources that locations and deities that are important in the ritual are not mentioned in the hymn (Clinton 1992). A site in Eleusis referred to as the Mirthless Rock was central to the ritual activity there, but it is never mentioned in the hymn. A deity by the name of Eubouleus was apparently believed to have accompanied Demeter's Persephone back from the underworld but is not mentioned either. Conversely, Demeter's attempt to make Demophon immortal, although connected to the general idea of gaining some kind of postmortem life through initiation, corresponds to nothing that is known of the concrete events that comprised the ritual.

The rituals that extended over a period of several days culminated in an initiation inside a temple in Eleusis, away from the public eye. Toward the very end of the text, the *Hymn to Demeter* alludes to the secrecy that shrouded this part of the activities:

Then she went to the kings, administrators of *themistes*,
and she showed them – to Triptolemos, to Diokles, driver of horses,
to powerful Eumolpos and to Keleos, leader of the people [*lâoi*] –
she revealed to them the way to perform the sacred rites, and she pointed out
  the ritual to all of them
– the holy ritual, which it is not at all possible to ignore, to find out about,
or to speak out. The great awe of the gods holds back any speaking out.

(Homeric Hymn to Demeter, 2018, lines 473–9)

The command to keep the mysteries secret was taken very seriously. In evidence is the sheer fact that the written sources about the events at Eleusis span a millennium and that vast numbers of people were initiated, yet we know little of what actually took place inside the sanctuary with any degree of certainty.

These examples illustrate how different modern textual sources are when compared to sources from antiquity, even taking into account that the vicissitudes of historical transmission mean most ancient texts are lost to us. A vast amount of evidence documents the details of modern religions; a situation like that of Mithraism, where nobody records the details of rituals and of their accompanying myths, is almost unthinkable in our own time. The very different forms of dissemination of information have also made it nearly impossible for movements that wish to keep secrets to restrict access to information. An illustrative modern-day parallel to the mysteries of antiquity is the Xenu myth of Scientology. This new religious movement is roughly organized as an ascending scale of stages and courses, where information imparted to those who reach the uppermost levels is supposed to remain confidential. Scientologists who reach a level called OT III are given access to a narrative that tells the story of how, in bygone times, a galactic ruler by the name of Xenu killed millions of beings from the various planets that he ruled over by means of hydrogen bombs (Rothstein 2009). The reason we know the plot of the Xenu myth – but can only speculate about many details of the Eleusinian mysteries – is that attempts to prevent outsiders from gaining access to the former have failed abysmally. The plot, initially disclosed by disgruntled former Scientology members, has been summarized or retold in detail in books, in articles, and on the Internet. It has been analyzed by scholars and ridiculed in an episode of the animated show *South Park*. A Wikipedia article provides interested readers with a detailed account of the myth (https://en.wikipedia.org/wiki/Xenu). By contrast, only hints of the initiatory secrets of ancient mystery religions were ever divulged.

Some Textual Genres in Antiquity

We shall in due course return to the presence in the ancient world of Jewish, Christian, and other religious currents that set out their doctrines and rituals in a corpus of sanctified writings. Although many religious currents of the time were not focused on a canonical corpus, it should be noted that we do have numerous texts from the Greco-Roman world representing many different genres. A few examples will illustrate how diverse and vast the mass of religious texts is.

A substantial number of works record the myths and rituals of Greco-Roman antiquity. Given the social context of literacy, much of this body of texts consists of literary renderings and learned speculation. In his work *Metamorphoses* (not to be confused with Apuleius's novel by that name), composed toward the end of the last century BCE, Ovid (43 BCE–17 CE) presents a loosely arranged sequence of myths that deal with the supernatural transformations of their protagonists, poetically rewritten in hexameter verse. Myths are linked to the Roman ritual calendar in another of Ovid's poetic works, *Fasti*. Here, the mythological and historical origins of communally celebrated rituals are given, ordered in chronological sequence throughout the first half of the year. For whatever reason, the work as it has come down to us does not continue with the six last months.

Texts from antiquity also reveal a curiosity about the religions of other people, often reinterpreted in terms of what is already known to the author and his presumed audience. At the core of much of this reinterpretation lies the kind of identification of foreign deities with those of the Greco-Roman pantheon mentioned in the previous section. When Tacitus (56–120 CE) in his *Germania* briefly mentions the religions of the Germanic peoples, he asserts that "Of the gods, they give a special worship to Mercury, to whom on certain days they count even the sacrifice of human life lawful. Hercules and Mars they appease with such animal life as is permissible. A section of the Suebi sacrifices also to Isis" (Tacitus, *Germania*, IX). Based on similarities between these characters as they were envisaged in Roman lore and what we know of ancient Germanic religion, scholars have tentatively surmised that Tacitus may have used the name Mercury to designate the Germanic Wodan/Odin and Mars as a Roman label for Tiw/Tyr, and that Hercules may be Donar/Thor, but they conclude that the identification of Isis remains mysterious.[15]

The problems of assessing the value of such descriptions as sources for understanding the religion of the Germanic peoples is apparent from the fact that the statement about Mercury as the main god is found almost verbatim in Caesar's (100 BCE–44 BCE) description of the religion of a different ethnic group, the Gauls, in his book *The Gallic War* (6,17.1). Did Tacitus merely quote

---

[15] For a detailed discussion of this passage with ample references to earlier studies, see Schuhmann 2009: 275–90.

a well-known literary trope? Did he fit what he knew about the Germanic pantheon into a preexisting mold? Or did he record an actual structural similarity between the Gallic and Germanic pantheons? Tacitus's description is terse and gives the reader few clues as to how he arrived at his understanding.

A more complex reinterpretation that provides a clearer view of how the unfamiliar could be seen through the lens of the familiar can be found in Plutarch's retelling of the myth of Isis and Osiris in his eponymous *Isis and Osiris*. Plutarch's discussion is so thoroughly Hellenized that, despite its lengthy rendition of an Egyptian myth and its description of Egyptian ritual practices, it has been characterized as "one of the foremost sources for second century Platonism" rather than as a source documenting Egyptian religion (Berchman 2007: 278). In Plutarch's perspective, true wisdom is provided by a philosophical understanding of the myth and of the ritual actions. Why, for instance, did Egyptian priests shave their heads and wear clothes made of linen? Plutarch's answer (*Isis and Osiris* 5, 352 f) is that these are symbols of purity, an interpretation he supports by quoting a passage from Plato's *Phaedrus*. How the Egyptians themselves may have understood these matters appears to be of little or no consequence. Similarly, elements in the myth of Isis that do not lend themselves to philosophical interpretation – that is, as a symbolic representation of Plutarch's Middle Platonic cosmology – are explicitly expunged from his retelling as too "barbaric" (*Isis and Osiris* 2, 358 e).

As the brief discussion of Plutarch's work shows, his fascination with Egypt was infused with a desire to appropriate and reinterpret Egyptian culture in a way that made sense to a highly literate and philosophically educated audience. Cultural appropriation also took place at the other end of the social spectrum, as exemplified in texts that provide instructions for carrying out rituals meant to attract a person of the opposite sex or to give one the upper hand in a competitive sport; in short, how to perform magic. These texts typically include instructions for manufacturing various objects necessary to carry out the magical ritual, spells to be recited and written, hymns, and sequences of mysterious-looking characters, palindromes, and the names of the supernatural beings one wishes to involve in the ritual act. An example of such a text from Roman Egypt provides elaborate instructions on how to make another person irresistibly attracted to the person who carries out the magical ritual (Papyri Graecae Magicae IV, 296–466). Two small figurines are to be crafted, showing an aggressive and dominant male standing over a submissive female. Various entities are summoned by uttering spells containing their names. Some of these beings have names, such as Persephone and Ereschigal, that are familiar from various religions of the region, whereas others, such as Phōkentazepseu, are presumably strictly part of the magicians' repertoire and are referred to by mysterious sequences of letters. Rhetorically, magicians who utter these words increase their potency until they assume the role of an all-powerful deity able to command these entities at will:

> I adjure you, god of the dead, whether male or female, by [long list of names]; do not fail, god of the dead, to heed my commands and names, but just arouse yourself from the repose which holds you, whoever you are, whether male or female, and go to every place, into every quarter, into every house, and attract her to me and with a spell keep her from eating and drinking, and do not allow her to accept for pleasure the attempt of another man, not even that of her husband, just that of mine. (Papyri Graecae Magicae IV, 361–76)

Once the person whose sexual submissiveness is ritually ensured has succumbed to the powers of these chthonic beings, they are released by the magician and can go back to rest. The text concludes with a hymn to the Greek sun god Helios, composed in a poetic style markedly different from the sometimes very graphic descriptions of the preceding sections.

The existence of such anonymously penned magical recipes contrasts with the official opprobrium against many such practices expressed in legal sources and in ancient texts on magic written by the intelligentsia of Greco-Roman society. Other rituals considered too foreign, such as some elements of the cult of the Great Goddess or Kybele, are also described by some authors of the period in strongly derogatory terms. We will return to the issue of how boundaries were drawn between acceptable religion and other forms of ritual practice in Section 4.

Canon Formation and the Attribution of Textual Authority

As we have noted, the idea of a closed canon of texts is particularly associated in antiquity with the Jewish and Christian traditions.[16] The concept became prototypical for other text-based religions, and competing religions – including Manichaeism, Mandaeism, and, later, Islam – also established their own selection of sacred writings.

The historical process of canon formation can be difficult to follow, not least because a religious movement that promotes a particular selection of texts as sacred can disregard or actively suppress the memory of how human agency was involved in shaping a putatively sacrosanct collection. The problematic state of the sources means the question of how a canon establishing the limits of the Hebrew Bible came into being remains a topic of considerable scholarly disagreement, and there is no consensus regarding when the process was

---

[16] On the concept of canon, see Smith 1982. On canonical texts in new religions, see Hammer and Rothstein 2012 and Gallagher 2014.

essentially completed (Lim 2013). We are on somewhat safer ground when it comes to understanding the broad outlines of how a New Testament canon emerged.[17] Roughly two or three decades after the death of Jesus, the first texts were written that document the existence of a Christ-centered group – the letters of Paul, usually dated roughly 50–60 CE. Soon thereafter, Christians of the most diverse persuasions composed works purportedly documenting the life of Jesus, the doctrines Christians should believe in, and much else besides. When an imperial power imposed an orthodoxy, this was not least done by setting boundaries between "true" gospels and texts that should be rejected. A passage from Paul's Epistle to the Galatians (1:9) points ahead at the intense efforts that would unfold to discredit various books as unworthy of scriptural status: "If anybody is preaching to you a gospel other than what you accepted, let them be under God's curse!" The process lasted some 300 years: the first mention of a Christian canon that matches the set of New Testament texts as known today is a list compiled in 367 CE by the bishop of Alexandria, Athanasius (298–373 CE).

The emergence of this canon can be seen as a result of a perceived need to distance oneself from other forms of Christianity that promoted other sets of texts. Marcion (ca. 85–ca. 160) understood the descriptions of the deity in the Hebrew Bible/Old Testament to be so different from the god of the Christians that he concluded they were two distinct entities. Christians, he concluded, should reject the texts of the Jewish corpus, and the only books they should rely on are the gospel of Luke and ten Pauline letters.[18] Other forms of Christianity gave special status to a larger set of texts than what would become the canonical set espoused by the emergent orthodoxy. Based on the preaching and prophetic utterances of Montanus (second century) and of a number of his associates, various revelatory messages, often apocalyptic in nature, became the foundation for a set of new sacred texts for a Montanist movement. The opposition to the Montanists generated a more general distrust of prophetic and apocalyptic texts and a move toward defining an accepted body of writings that would exclude such works.[19] Members of various Christian movements thus defined their identities in terms of the books they regarded as authoritative, and the twenty-seven books eventually compiled as the New Testament were the collection of the movement that ultimately came to dominate Christianity.

Religious insiders understand the canon's sacredness as an unquestioned fact, while the issue of why a particular set of texts was selected and compiled is

---

[17] The description here is based on Kyrtatas 2010.

[18] On Marcion and his selection of texts, see Räisänen 2005.

[19] On the Montanist movement, see Marjanen 2005. For their role in delimiting an orthodox canon, see also Metzger 1987: 99–106.

usually of no great concern. If they consider the matter at all, concepts such as divine inspiration are more readily invoked than any references to the kind of contingent processes we have summarized. More generally, the special status of particular texts tends to derive from a small set of legitimizing claims that may have a tenuous connection, if any at all, to historical events. A particular text can be accorded an exceptional significance because the author is ascribed exceptional qualities. He – for authors of religious texts in antiquity were overwhelmingly men – could, for instance, base his claim to authority on his contact with a suprahuman realm. Paul claimed to have met Jesus in a vision, Mani (to whom we shall return) had revelations, as did the anonymous author of the Hermetic treatise *Poimandres*. Other texts are seen as particularly significant because their authors are singled out for their purported role as eyewitnesses to the events described, or at least for having lived and written at a time close to the events depicted. Later texts could be retrojected in time by being attributed to such key individuals. More generally, pseudepigrapha – texts ascribed to other, more prestigious authors than the people who actually wrote them – were common. Of the thirteen epistles in the New Testament supposedly written by Paul, most scholars are convinced that six were actually written by later authors. The gospels of Matthew and John were not composed by the apostles traditionally believed to have written them, but they carry the names of people whose proximity to Jesus and his time gave legitimacy to the texts.

Authority-bolstering claims about the (real or presumed) author are often put forth in what one can call a secondary textual layer. Paul's epistles are special because he had a vision of Christ on the road to Damascus. In several of those letters, this claim to authority is based on Paul's brief references to his visionary experience in passages such as 1 Corinthians 15:8 and Galatians 1:11–16. The book of Acts relates the events in greater detail and no fewer than three times, adding a more elaborate narrative to support the claim that Paul was the recipient of a divine vision. Acts 9:1–19 tells the story of how Saul, the enraged persecutor of the followers of Jesus who would later change his name to Paul, sees a light from heaven and is struck to the ground. A voice, identifying itself as Jesus, tells Saul to enter the city of Damascus and await instructions. The veracity of the vision is narratively confirmed and its meaning elucidated by having Paul's companions also hear the voice, by the temporary blindness the vision causes in him, and by the testimony of a man by the name of Ananias who receives a vision confirming that Jesus has selected Paul to henceforth be his "chosen instrument to take my message to the Gentiles and to kings, as well as to the people of Israel." Ananias cures Paul's blindness by laying his hands on him, a further narrative confirmation the sequence of events is truly supernatural.

Similar ways of gaining authority can be found in religions outside the Christian context. In the third century of the Common Era, a missionizing religion was founded by a prophetic figure from the town of Seleucia-Ctesiphon in Mesopotamia by the name of Mani (216–77 CE).[20] The Manichaean religion had a canonical set of texts attributed to Mani himself, but due to the persecution of the Manichaeans by its competitors, not least Christianity, only fragments of this scriptural canon remain. The doctrines of the new creed are nevertheless well known from other texts. In short, two cosmic principles, often presented in terms of a dualism between light and darkness or good and evil, were once separate but are now intermingled and fight for dominance. In the present epoch, the principle of light is subjected to suffering because it is trapped in matter, which is equated with evil. A future epoch awaits when, aided by the efforts of the Manichaeans, light will once more be separated from its material imprisonment. Historians of religion have seen Mani's teachings as a confluence of ideas from a host of other traditions known to him. The perspective of the Manichaean sources, however, is quite different, namely that Mani received revelations, in particular from an angelic being identified as "the twin." Mani's visions resulted in his distancing himself from the religion he had been brought up in – a group known as the Elkasaites – and developing his own views.

Mani's revelatory visions are described in a compilation of biographical passages recorded in a diminutive manuscript measuring 4.4 by 3.5 centimeters, written in Greek and known as the *Cologne Mani-Codex*.[21] The text also recounts miraculous events that purport to show the exalted nature of the prophet and illustrate some of the basic doctrines of Manichaeism: trees being cut and plants being harvested speak to Mani of their suffering, thus illustrating the basic idea that the living soul trapped even in such lowly matter as plants suffers. Besides being a record of narratives about Mani's personal background that would legitimize his role as prophet and creator of a new religion, the book's small size suggests it may have been intended to be worn as an amulet.

In theory, at least, this process of supporting the authority of a text through other textual materials could continue in any number of iterations: the reliability and authority of the supporting, secondary textual materials could in turn be confirmed by tertiary narratives, and so forth. As we have seen, the story of Paul's vision in Acts 9 involves a brief but important appearance of a person by the name of Ananias, of whom little is told in the biblical text. His role is significant enough for a supporting biography to emerge: his status as a saintly

---

[20] On Mani's biography, see Gnoli 1987.

[21] The University of Cologne maintains a website with useful information and an extensive bibliography of scholarly work on this text at https://papyri.uni-koeln.de/features/mani-kodex.

person who dies as a martyr is elaborated upon in later legends, a cult of his relics is instituted, and a structure in Damascus is identified as his house. Ananias is thus transformed from little more than a name to the truly worthy recipient of a vision that ratifies Paul's key role for the young movement. In practice, the quest for legitimacy reaches an end point, with a number of crucial claims functioning as unquestioned and perhaps ultimately unquestionable axioms that have no further support or are supported in circular fashion. A biblical passage about Paul relies on the mention of Ananias to gain credibility and Ananias in turn is deemed an important focus of religious interest because he is mentioned in a biblical passage. The *Cologne Mani-Codex* supports the claim that Mani had received direct revelations from a transcendent source by referring to quotes collected by earlier generations of Manichaean authorities in which Mani stated he had had these experiences. Whether by reaching a rock bottom of axiomatic claims or by circular forms of legitimacy, a text deemed sacred can ultimately be accorded an agency and a voice of its own. New generations of readers take as a basic fact that the text conveys truths, and their role is to work out, in more or less inventive ways, precisely how its assertions are correct.

The Role of Commentaries and Novel Interpretations

Once a religious community has decided on which texts are to be considered sacred and special, the set of selected narratives, descriptions of rituals, and doctrinal statements cannot easily be changed. Although one might suspect that the existence of a fixed set of writings forces a considerable degree of conservatism upon the community, religions based upon a scriptural canon are continually revised in order to adapt to changing circumstances or to suit the purposes of various groups and individuals. The canon functions as a kind of official source from which these individuals and groups can select different subsets that make sense to them and can conversely accord little if any interest to other parts of the canon. Commentaries and interpretations also open up a textual canon that would otherwise seem closed and can subject it to readings that will harmonize seeming contradictions, generate new understandings of the text, and make it relevant to current concerns. Biblical passages gain new meanings when they are read from a later vantage point: hence, texts from the Hebrew Bible are Christianized by being retrospectively read as foretelling events of Christian soteriological history, and untold numbers of Christian writers will elaborate their own versions of such interpretive innovations.

Texts that purport to comment upon previous texts can use these older sources as malleable raw materials that can be reinterpreted almost beyond recognition.

Several manuscripts that form part of a collection of papyrus codices found near the town of Nag Hammadi in Upper Egypt document the religious ideas of groups of people – Gnostics, to use a term that has become controversial – who understood biblical narratives in ways that will seem distinctly unfamiliar to most modern readers.[22] A straightforward reading of the first chapter of Genesis is that the deity who plays the central role in the narrative is the creator of the cosmos. Several times during the process of creation, the deity sees that what has been fashioned "is good." These passages raise the question of how a supremely powerful god can shape a world in which there is so much suffering and claim it is good. An answer can be found in Nag Hammadi texts such as the *Apocryphon of John* and the *Hypostasis of the Archons*: the being that has created the world of matter in which we find ourselves cannot be the transcendent and benevolent god who created the spiritual world but must be a blind and arrogant lower deity. The world of matter functions as a prison in which we are trapped, but humans forget this fact and need to be awakened to the truth. When the serpent tempts Eve in the garden of Eden in Genesis 3:1–5, some Gnostic texts tells their readers that the real meaning of this passage is that the serpent imparted this insight to the first human beings. The references to the passages in Genesis are unmistakable, but the meaning the Gnostic texts find in the biblical sources is remarkably innovative.[23]

At the end of the period we are surveying in this Element, two important and immensely influential innovations had become fixtures of the religious landscape, namely the attribution of a special or sacred quality to certain texts and the role of interpretation and commentary in allowing these fixed texts to become relevant in new contexts. Innumerable religious innovations in our own time continue to rely on these twin mechanisms of textual transmission. On one hand, two millennia after the foundational writings of the Jesus movement were produced, new meanings continue to be eked out from their pages. These span a broad spectrum, from reactions to new cultural and social contexts to reinterpretations that depart radically from previous understandings of the text. Interpretive innovations that characterize contemporary readings of biblical narratives include the ways in which various branches of Christianity have attempted to come to grips with the dominant role of the sciences, whether by relegating parts of the biblical account to the status of myths or, on the contrary, by insisting the Bible is inerrant and does not contain even a single factual error.

---

[22] The term "Gnosticism" has been critiqued for encompassing a variety of quite distinct religious currents; the tendency to lump these currents together under a shared label has its origins in heresiological literature (cf. Williams 1996; King 2003). For the sake of convenience, we maintain the imperfect designation in this brief discussion.

[23] For a discussion of how biblical texts were reinterpreted in Gnostic literature, see Pearson 2007.

At the radical end of the spectrum, we find creative readers who have, for instance, argued that the gospels' narratives about Jesus are symbolic allusions to the descent into human shape of a spiritual entity emanating from the sun, or that various passages in the Bible record the visit of aliens from outer space in past times.[24]

On the other hand, numerous new textual corpora have become regarded as special or even sacrosanct by members of various new religions. The Church of Jesus Christ of Latter-day Saints, for instance, explicitly designates a corpus of four works as scripture: the Bible, the Book of Mormon, Doctrine and Covenants, and the Pearl of Great Price. The canonical status of the Book of Mormon is evident from its language, reminiscent of the style of the King James Bible, and its division into books, each of which, like those of the Bible, is subdivided into chapters and verses. As with older texts accorded a particularly exalted status, a secondary textual layer provides a legitimizing narrative. According to this account, a series of extraordinary events led Joseph Smith Jr. to gain access to a text engraved on gold plates and translate its Reformed Egyptian characters by supernatural means into the English text that constitutes the Book of Mormon. Another example of a set of texts that has gained canonical status is the collected works of the founder of Scientology, L. Ron Hubbard. The secondary textual layer is in this case a hagiography that presents Hubbard as an unparalleled genius. His writings are perhaps the most extravagant example of a corpus treated as a sacred collection. The Church of Scientology deems them so important that they have been placed in titanium boxes inside a vault constructed in a remote location in New Mexico so every word Hubbard wrote will be preserved for posterity.[25]

3 Holy Men, Charismatic Leaders, and Religious Entrepreneurs

As we have seen, regional globalization increased after the military campaigns of Alexander the Great in the late fourth century BCE brought many different cultures into contact, and as Rome eventually began its expansion, the process continued. People engaged in trade, administration, or military activities tied vast areas together and became citizens of the world, and as boundaries were transcended and cultural exchanges intensified, religions met and influenced each other. No single philosophy, no single ideology, no single religion ruled. Rome, of course, claimed absolute political authority and insisted everyone

---

[24] On the gospels interpreted as records of a solar myth, see Hammer 2019; for the purported references to space aliens in the Bible, see Hammer and Swartz 2021.

[25] The existence of this vault was revealed by several newspapers, one of the earliest being the *Washington Post*; see washingtonpost.com/wp-dyn/content/article/2005/11/26/AR200511260 1065.html.

should abide by Roman laws. Nevertheless, people were free, within rather diffuse boundaries, to engage in any of the many religious activities on offer. Some of these options were associated with specific individuals who formulated and disseminated new messages. Although most of the men and women who introduced new religious ideas and practices in the Hellenistic and Roman periods will no doubt forever remain unknown to us, we do have accounts of several religious entrepreneurs whose innovative claims were supported by their alleged extraordinary or even divine qualities.

The existence of numerous such figures can, for instance, be inferred from the gospel of Matthew, a text composed in the late first century CE in which Jesus is portrayed as an aspiring and self-confident prophet who utters this warning against his competitors on the turbulent religious scene:

> Beware of false prophets, who come to you in sheep's clothing but inwardly are ravenous wolves. You will know them by their fruits. Are grapes gathered from thorns, or figs from thistles? In the same way, every good tree bears good fruit, but the bad tree bears bad fruit. A good tree cannot bear bad fruit, nor can a bad tree bear good fruit. Every tree that does not bear good fruit is cut down and thrown into the fire. Thus you will know them by their fruits. (Matthew 7:15–20)

This trope sets the scene for a Christian distrust of other religions that has endured through two millennia. The claim that religious leaders promoting other gods are sinister and deceitful is central to many branches of Christianity even today and is particularly well known from the debate on new religious movements that numerous Christian writers have branded as sects and cults (see, e.g., Cowan 2023). This condemnation of other religious messages, however, was not a prevalent attitude in Hellenistic and Roman society. The Jews, present in most corners of the Hellenistic-Roman world, represented a rare point of view by claiming that there was only one god worthy of worship, namely their own (Gruen 2016: 22). Most people in the vast Roman world embraced the idea that there were numerous gods and that one could relate to any number of them. Some gods could be worshipped by anybody, others were the focus of devotion by initiates, but the fact that other people venerated other gods did not cause much concern. In this religious landscape, there were few barriers against individuals introducing new religious ideas and practices. Those who were successful attracted other people who could continue the work started by these religious innovators, proselytize, organize adherents, and elaborate on the theological implications of the founder's message. Examples are Paul of Tarsus, who ardently promoted the Jesus movement; the Roman senator Publius Mummius Sisenna Rutilianus (second century CE), who invested his personal credibility in the Glycon cult; and the Greek author Philostratus (170–ca. 245 CE), who was an avid defender of the prophet Apollonius of Tyana (see later in this section). If support was provided by the political elite, such religious innovations could become fixtures of the cultural landscape. Imperial Rome saw the conversion of what was at first a striking novelty, the deification of the emperor, into a cornerstone of Roman religion, and at the end of the period we are considering here, two emperors, Constantine and Theodosius, played key roles in transforming Christianity from a controversial movement into an enduring and powerful religion.

In this section, we will present and discuss in chronological order a small sample of religious innovators. Texts written by religious insiders typically insist on the uniquely elevated nature of the person they revere. By contrast, religious competitors describe their opponents in exceptionally hostile terms. Due to the patchy and extremely biased nature of most sources, our knowledge about these individuals and the groups or movements that arose around them is limited, but as we will see, some commonalities can nevertheless be discerned, since they were part of the shared cultural context we presented in the first section. The picture that emerges is comparable to that of religious visionaries and entrepreneurs in other historical periods including the present (cf. Bilde 2013; Rothstein in press).

One of the most salient culturally determined traits can be mentioned at the outset. The gender imbalance of our five cases reflects the fact that, with very few exceptions, religious innovators in the Hellenistic and Roman periods were males. Women certainly appear everywhere in our material, but far more often as participants in traditional religious practices than as religious forerunners. Greek women participated in various festivals and could even become priests, but these activities were placed within a mainstream understanding of their religious roles (Dillon 2002). They joined some of the cults introduced during the period surveyed here, but to the extent that the sources afford any glimpse of their religious lives, they were participants rather than innovators. Roman women also were present in religious life, but ideally in ways that served the aim of preserving the social order (Takács 2008). The Vestals of Rome held an important role in the religious sphere, but they were not the creators of the cult in which they officiated, and through the centuries they were victims of political manipulation as much as powerful caretakers of a state institution. Similarly, the cult for Bona Dea, an all-female institution, was under state control and was not a new religion. The nature of our textual evidence, documents written by men who lived in societies permeated by intensely patriarchal norms, may, of course, skew our view of the potential role of women as religious innovators. To the extent that there may have been more numerous female religious entrepreneurs in antiquity, barely any trace of them has survived. Among the few exceptions are female prophetic figures in early Christianity. The Montanist movement (discussed earlier in this Element) was named after its male founder and prophet Montanus, but two female recipients of divine messages, Priscilla and Maximilla, were immensely influential members of a triad of leaders. Such examples, however, are few and far between.

Augustus (63 BCE–14 CE) and the Imperial Cult

Among all the religious innovations in antiquity, the introduction of the Roman imperial cult was one of the most important.[26] It was initiated from above and was enforced as an all-embracing framework designed to consolidate and unite the widespread and extremely variegated empire. In a multireligious society like that of the Romans, this new, overarching religious practice could project political power even to the most remote outskirts of the realm. The impetus for this development may have come from territories the Romans had recently conquered, where people found it hard to submit to a ruler who did not accept offerings since their kings had always been associated with the gods. The new concept had deep roots in the ancient sacred kingdoms of the Middle East and in Hellenistic traditions that had divinized rulers since Alexander the Great and had evolved into the elaborate cults of the various rulers of the Ptolemaic dynasty mentioned earlier. In its Roman guise, it may have been a version of these concepts that was adapted to the religious and political reality of the empire, or an extension of an existing Roman understanding of a cult focusing on a god as an acknowledgment of the higher status of the deity rather than of an essential difference between gods and humans (Gradel 2002: 27–32). In either case, this religious innovation involved developing well-known features of the religious landscape into a new shape.

The imperial cult can be seen as an expansion of the open-ended Roman religious system. New gods had been introduced on many occasions, and Rome's multireligious, polytheistic society was perfectly capable of including yet another divinity. What was special about the imperial cult was its political nature, effectively making not only the emperor himself but also his office divine. It was mandatory for all to participate in it; refusing to do so was tantamount to committing the treasonous act of rejecting the political order.

---

[26] Our case studies throughout this section are based on descriptions and analyses readily available in the relevant scholarly literature. For the imperial cult, see the detailed analysis in Gradel 2002 and the brief summary in Herz 2007, as well as the extensive literature referred to in those works. On the deification of Caesar, see in particular Gradel 2002: 54–72; on that of Augustus, see Gradel 2002: 109–16.

On the other hand, people were free to have other religious affiliations as long as they took part in the cult of the emperor.

The divinization of the emperor was a gradual process. Julius Caesar had for many years promoted himself as a godlike person, and he was shortly before his assassination in 44 BCE elevated to fully divine rank as *Divus Julius*. Only over the next years, however, did his deification occasion the construction of a temple and the appointment of a priest to carry out the cult dedicated to him. The deification of Caesar paved the way for the divinization of his adopted son Octavian, later known as Augustus; if his adoptive father was a god, how could Augustus be anything less?

According to legend, a host of divinatory signs had confirmed Augustus's status. In his biography of Augustus, part of a set of twelve biographies completed shortly after 120 CE, the Roman author Suetonius (69–after 122 CE) writes:

> In ancient days, when a part of the wall of Velitrae had been struck by lightning, the prediction was made that a citizen of that town would one day rule the world.
>
> According to Julius Marathus, a few months before Augustus was born a portent was generally observed at Rome, which gave warning that nature was pregnant with a king for the Roman people.
>
> Again, as he was taking the auspices in his first consulship, twelve vultures appeared to him, as to Romulus, and when he slew the victims, the livers within all of them were found to be doubled inward at the lower end, which all those who were skilled in such matters unanimously declared to be an omen of a great and happy future. (Suetonius, *The Deified Augustus*, 94.2, 92.3, and 95)

Augustus was careful not to make his identity as a god the object of a state cult, but there were ways of promoting the view of him as divine through iconography, rituals, and narratives. A famous statue (Augustus of Prima Porta) presents him as a human being, but with hints of his superior nature: He is barefoot, a feature otherwise characteristic of the gods, and accompanied by a small Cupid riding on a dolphin, a symbol suggesting his family ties to Venus and thus his divine lineage.

Although the creation of an official cult seems to have been out of the question, Augustus could be worshipped in numerous other ritual settings. No later than 7 BCE, the veneration of the *Genius Augusti* was introduced, a term that in Augustus's days seems to have denoted a kind of personal protective deity or guardian spirit. By sacrificing to the *Genius* at one of the many altars dedicated to the cult, the broader community of Romans would serve as cocreators of the emperor's divinity, confirming Max Weber's basic insight (in, e.g., Weber 1968: 18–27) that charisma is a quality attributed to a person by their followers. A ruler aspiring to being cast as a god hence needs active ritual participants to elevate him to this level of religious prominence.

Augustus's autobiographical (or, perhaps, auto-hagiographical) narrative, the appropriately named *Res Gestae Divi Augusti* (*Deeds of the Divine Augustus*), is reminiscent of the aretalogy genre presented in the preceding section. Inscriptions with this text were after his death displayed at his tomb and at temples throughout the empire dedicated to his cult, glorifying his accomplishments, and reminding his devotees of the many reasons for honoring him posthumously as they had during his lifetime:

> I was named Augustus by senatorial decree, and the doorposts of my house were publicly clothed with laurels, and a civic crown was fastened above my doorway, and a golden shield was set up in the Julian senate house; through an inscription on this shield was declared that the Roman senate and people were giving it to me because of my valour, clemency, justice, and piety. (*Res Gestae Divi Augusti*, 32)

One divine emperor, of course, does not constitute an institution, but more divinized rulers were to follow, and during Augustus's reign and beyond, the new cult was methodically consolidated and extended. The image of the ruler, for instance, was distributed to every corner of the empire, and people were instructed to perform sacrifices before it. In a sense, the many visual representations served as extensions of the emperor himself, who by means of reliefs, statues, and busts became approachable to local populations. In fact, whenever a new ruler or political figure was promoted, iconographic representations were a common means of doing so. A probably unsolvable question is whether such statues, reliefs, or paintings were experienced as depictions or if they were understood as an actual manifestation of the divine. Perhaps the ritual was simply a set of prescribed actions unaccompanied by any particular conceptual framework or interpretation (cf. Gradel 2002: 1–4).

Imperial deification was significantly extended by the third emperor Caligula's (12–41 CE) decision to grant posthumous divine status to his sister and perhaps incestuous consort, Julia Drusilla (16–38 CE), who died quite young. Diva Drusilla Panthea's deification was, according to art historian Susan Wood, the emperor's "attempt to make the best of dynastic disaster by keeping her in public imagery as a symbolic mother figure of the Julians" (Wood 1995: 457). Drusilla never produced the male heir Caligula wanted, but her potential to bear Julian children could at least be celebrated. Wood also notes that provincial coinages indicate that the consecration of Drusilla was in fact quite popular. Accordingly, she sees Caligula's deification of his sister as a rational decision rather than as the expression of the emperor's insanity, the explanation many earlier writers proposed. According to some sources, Caligula had strategically promoted himself as a god by publicly posing with the symbols and epithets of gods and demigods such as Hercules, Apollo, and Mercury. If these generally rather hostile accounts are accurate, his ambition of deifying his sister should probably also be seen as an extension of his conviction that he himself was a god.

As the example of Caligula and his sister illustrates, the imperial cult was, like all religious phenomena, open to change over time. The extension of divinization to members of the imperial family had been explicitly ruled out in the early stages of the imperial cult but could also, after Caligula's time, become a strategic part of it. Tiberius, the successor to Augustus, was not only reticent about his own deification but opposed that of his mother Livia. However, in 42 CE, Claudius (10 BCE–54 CE), the successor to Caligula, ordered Livia deified as Diva Augusta, hence strengthening his own connection to the ruling dynasty by elevating his grandmother to the rank of a divinity.

Clearly, divine honors were given to people, dead or alive, for political purposes. As long as the general population participated in the cult, their opinion was probably a minor concern, and personal belief, a profoundly Christian notion of what a religion is all about, presumably mattered even less. The top-down imposition of the imperial cult and its strategic reformulation by successive rulers suggest this was not a new religion in the sense in which this term is usually understood – that is, as the result of a charismatic, prophetic figure gaining adherents – but a cultural innovation deliberately developed within a complex system in which there was no differentiation between religion and politics. Similarly, offshoots such as the separate cults to family members such as Livia or Drusilla did not arise through the usual mechanisms of diversification within a family of religions – for example, via schisms within an organization – but by the equally deliberate dedication of temples to these divinized individuals and the appointment of staff to oversee their cult. Nevertheless, sources indicate that at least in some parts of the Roman Empire, perhaps especially in regions where the idea of divine humans was already well established, ordinary people displayed behavior that indicates that suprahuman abilities were attributed to the ruler. Peter Herz (2007: 310) notes that Vespasian (9–79 CE) during a visit to Alexandria was met by sick people who expected him to be able to heal them by simply laying his hands on them.

By creating the foundational notions underlying the Roman cult of the divine emperor, Augustus took the culturally preexisting idea that some human beings were akin to gods by virtue of their elevated status to new heights and initiated a set of concepts and practices that endured until the demise of pagan religious culture. Another god-man from Augustus's time set in motion a course of events that would prove far more successful in the long run, as the legends told about him inspired the creation of the world's largest family of religions, Christianity.

Jesus of Nazareth (b. ca. 4 BCE–d. ca. 30 CE)

Compared to the sources documenting other religious innovators and charismatic leaders in antiquity, the corpus of texts that has become known as the New Testament is exceptional in both quantity and detail. Much of the collection consists of hagiographical accounts of the god-man Jesus of Nazareth and descriptions of how the early Jesus movement was organized and under what social and political conditions it came into being. One might expect this to make Jesus the best known of all ancient prophets and miracle workers and the early stages of the movement he inspired (or rather movements, as there were more than one) the best-known new religion of antiquity. The Jesus of the texts, however, is not identical to the Jesus of history but the product of the religious imagination. Scholars have for centuries tried to separate fact from fiction, but our task is easier than theirs. Although we do refer occasionally to what seem to be reasonably well-established historical facts, our main focus is what Jesus's followers attributed to him, namely that within a short span of time, they had come to see him as capable of miraculous feats, and that within the few decades that separate the earliest New Testament sources from the latest, some had even concluded he was in fact divine. As Bart Ehrman argues in his book *How Jesus Became God* (2014), the elevation of Jesus to superhuman and ultimately divine status was a gradual process, and different New Testament texts do not present him in the same terms. Religious insiders, by contrast, often read these accounts as parts of a coherent narrative about Jesus. The composite picture they can construct is that he was a deity from the beginning who took on human shape. His extraordinary status was evident from his ability to walk on water, magically multiply objects, pass through walls, communicate with evil powers, cast out demons, heal the sick, raise the dead, see into the future, transform matter, supernaturally cause trees to die, command the weather, overcome death, and ultimately ascend into the heavens.

The transformation of Jesus the apocalyptic preacher into Jesus the divine human seems to have been the result of a crisis in the group who followed his message. They saw in him a person who would soon fulfill their messianic expectations and usher in the kingdom of God. What happened instead, according to the textual accounts, was that he was handed over by the Jewish Sanhedrin to the Roman authorities, who sentenced him to death and had him crucified, a violent and humiliating death normally reserved for slaves and enemies of the state. A radical notion was introduced to counteract the cognitive dissonance caused by the clash between the messianic hope and the brutal execution of their leader: Jesus had, it was claimed, overcome death, left his grave, and lived among his followers for a period of forty days before returning to the realm of God the Father from where he had descended. After the resurrected Jesus had left his disciples, another divine figure, the Holy Spirit, came to inspire and empower the faithful. Ultimately, however, Jesus would return from his celestial abode, judge humankind, and create a new world for those found worthy. Seen from this perspective, his crucifixion was not a failure but a necessary part of a divine plan.

The gospel of John in particular presents Jesus as divine and has him proclaim that "Whoever has seen me has seen the Father" (14:9), state that "I and the Father are one" (10:30), and designate himself in the same way as God does in Exodus, namely "I am" (8:58). One reason for the success of this new understanding of Jesus was that the line between the human and divine dimensions was perceived as quite fluid. Indeed, "even among Jews at the time of Jesus there was not a sense of an absolute break, a complete divide, an unbridgeable chasm between the divine and the human" (Ehrman 2014: 83). The notion that the deity had taken on human form became the central idea of a new religious movement. The theological need to reconcile the insistence upon the monotheistic claims of Christianity and the divinity of its central figure over time led to innovative claims that departed fundamentally from Roman and Jewish ways of understanding the nature of the divine realm.

In the earliest phase of the Jesus movement, devotees would gather in private houses in order to meet and perform rituals. As the new religion spread, churches became the new venues for the cult. During the first century, the notion of *ecclesia*, the community of believers, became established. The devotees of Christ were like "one body," a spiritual elite uniquely destined for the world to come when their god would reappear from the divine realm. This sense of being set apart from others is established already in the New Testament corpus. Whereas other deities in the Hellenistic and Roman periods were typically part of a fluid religious culture in which multiple allegiances were commonplace, several passages in the New Testament texts insist Jesus is the only true deity. Jesus in the gospel of John (14:9) states that he is "the way, and the truth, and the life," and that "No one comes to the Father except through me" (14:5).

The ritual structure of the new religion in many ways resembled the mystery religions of the surrounding religious landscape. An initiation ritual, baptism, placed the devotee under Jesus's divine protection and allowed him or her access to the salvific ritual: a sacred meal, where bread and wine, magically transformed into the flesh and blood of Jesus, was consumed. By consuming their god, devotees aligned with him in his struggle against evil and his victory over death and were thus themselves promised eternal life. The gospel of John emphasizes the importance and perhaps even the literal nature of this act and explains how it separates those who understand its significance from those who do not:

> "Your fathers ate the manna in the wilderness, and they died. This is the bread that comes down from heaven, so that one may eat of it and not die. I am the living bread that came down from heaven. If anyone eats of this bread, he will live forever. And the bread that I will give for the life of the world is my flesh."
>
> The Jews then disputed among themselves, saying, "How can this man give us his flesh to eat?" So Jesus said to them, "Truly, truly, I say to you, unless you eat the flesh of the Son of Man and drink his blood, you have no life in you. Whoever feeds on my flesh and drinks my blood has eternal life, and I will raise him up on the last day. For my flesh is true food, and my blood is true drink. Whoever feeds on my flesh and drinks my blood abides in me, and I in him. As the living Father sent me, and I live because of the Father, so whoever feeds on me, he also will live because of me. This is the bread that came down from heaven, not like the bread the fathers ate, and died. Whoever feeds on this bread will live forever." (John 6:49–58)

There are also passages that hint that Jesus's teachings, like those of various mystery cults, were reserved for a restricted audience:

> Then the disciples came and asked him: "Why do you speak to them in parables?" He answered: "To you it has been given to know the secrets of the kingdom of heaven, but to them it has not been given . . . The reason I speak to them in parables is that 'seeing they do not perceive, and hearing they do not listen, nor do they understand'." (Matthew 13:10–14)

In the extracanonical gospel of Thomas, Jesus comes across even more distinctly as the purveyor of "secret words" only privileged insiders would be able to interpret.[27] The understanding that came to dominate was, however, rooted in the opposite belief, namely that the cult of Jesus should be made widely known to others. In Matthew 10:5–6, these others are still a restricted group of people. Jesus is quoted as enjoining his disciples to spread the message to the "lost sheep of the house of Israel" but not to Gentiles or Samaritans. The key textual passage that universalizes the message and that has been cited countless times to support a global proselytizing effort comes from a later passage in Matthew, where Jesus meets with his followers after his return from the dead:

---

[27] Gospel of Thomas, introductory passage and logion 1.

> When they saw him, they worshipped him; but some doubted. And Jesus
> came and said to them: "All authority in heaven and on earth has been given
> to me. Go therefore and make disciples of all nations, baptizing them in the
> name of the Father and of the Son and of the Holy Spirit, and teaching them to
> obey everything that I have commanded you." (Matthew 28:17–20)

As we will see in somewhat greater detail in Section 4, Christians were intermittently persecuted in Rome for three centuries, but in the fourth century, Christianity had become a uniquely powerful religious ideology. Political support and a firm conviction, based on this mythological narrative about the instructions given by the resurrected Jesus, ultimately led to the present situation where the innumerable Christian denominations together have more than 2 billion adherents.[28]

Apollonius of Tyana (b. ca. 40–d. ca. 120 CE)

According to Gregory J. Riley (2000), the stories crafted about Jesus were mythologically in line with those that surrounded the Greek heroes, who were presented as semidivine beings that accomplished marvelous feats. Religious stories are rarely radically new, but are usually a reformulation of older ideas, often in new contexts or in new combinations. It therefore comes as no surprise that similar narratives were told about other religious innovators as well. One such man was the first-century philosopher and religious teacher Apollonius from the town of Tyana in the Roman province of Cappadocia, in what is now central Turkey.[29] His life is not only close to that of Jesus in time but also resembles it in terms of the legendary elaborations presented in the sources. The narratives about the two individuals are remarkably alike, and it is not strange that their later followers would engage in theological disputes, each side promoting its own master. While the stories of Jesus the divine human being live on as a central part of the mythology of Christianity, there is no enduring religion based on the life and teachings of Apollonius. He is therefore mainly known to those who have a particular interest in pre-Christian prophetic figures, which, as we will see at the end of this case study, is a motley collection of people.

While pregnant, so the story goes, Apollonius's mother had a vision of the god of wisdom, Proteus, who told her the child she was about to deliver would be a manifestation of Proteus himself. She gave birth under extraordinary

---

[28] The Statista database, drawing on data from the Pew Research Center, states that in 2015, 31 percent of the world's population comprised Christians (www-statista-com.proxy1-bib.sdu.dk/chart/25572/worlds-largest-religious-groups-over-time). The very rough figure of more than 2 billion is based on the world population in that year (7.3 billion) and at the time of writing (8 billion).

[29] For a substantial and source-critical investigation of what can be deduced about the historical figure of Apollonius of Tyana, see Dzielska 1986.

circumstances. A great portent was seen: a bolt of lightning was suspended in midair and returned to the sky without ever reaching the ground. It was concluded that the infant was in fact the son of Zeus, the great god. When Apollonius came of age, he was not only a religious preacher but performed miracles such as healing the sick, casting out demons, and raising the dead, and the rumors of his accomplishments were many. When he died, a choir of unseen girls sang: "Hasten thou from earth, hasten thou to Heaven, hasten" (Philostratus, *The Life of Apollonius of Tyana*, 8, 30), and so Apollonius found his rightful place among the gods in heaven, where he still lives. After his death, legend has it, he appeared to one of his followers to assure him (and others), that he had returned from the dead.

The extraordinary life of Apollonius is narrated by Philostratus, a disciple who wrote a biography in eight books, *The Life of Apollonius of Tyana*, in the first third of the third century CE – that is, at an even greater chronological remove from the protagonist of his story than the books of the New Testament were from the life of Jesus. According to Philostratus himself, a number of earlier books about the sage were consulted in order to compile the *Life*, but the obvious legendary accretions of the biography and the apologetic agenda of the author show we need to be as skeptical when evaluating their historicity as we should be in the case of the New Testament accounts. Philostratus's overall credibility, or lack thereof, can be gauged from the fact that the source that he claimed had given him the most important information about the revered teacher was written by one of Apollonius's closest disciples, Damis. The problem is that Damis probably never existed but was a literary fiction Philostratus created. From a historical perspective, Apollonius was presumably an itinerant Pythagorean philosopher with no intention of changing the polytheistic nature of Roman society. Beyond a few such basic facts, scholars have struggled to reconstruct anything more concrete about the "real" Apollonius, but our task is also in this case a different one, namely to give an idea of what others attributed to him.

Philostratus's biography tells us Apollonius was a man of supreme virtue and intelligence whose piety was demonstrated by his visit to innumerable sacred sites during his extensive travels. He appeared in temples, where he offered his wisdom free of charge and made himself available to public servants and religious administrators. He would engage with ordinary people and give them advice on how to live and think and would serve as a peacemaker and mediator. Miracles of the kind summarized earlier are in Philostratus's rendition not attributed to divine intervention or to Apollonius being a deity. Rather, he is presented as having a kind of natural command over such things as the weather. According to Wendy Cotter, the understanding was "that Apollonius is recognized by nature due to his own holy life, not through a deity's empowerment" (Cotter 2010: 227). In that sense, he was, of course, cast quite differently from Jesus, who was within a few decades after his death seen as either a god-sent messenger or a god himself. Toward the end of his life, Apollonius was, according to Philostratus, accused of posing as a god without being one in fact, and a trial was held to protect the state against his allegedly subversive activities.

As we have noted, little is known about the historical figure, but the tropes we find in Philostratus's hagiography resemble those associated with other individuals who were elevated to the rank of heroes and deities, and there is evidence that Apollonius, like them, was the focus of religious devotion. A century after his death, a shrine was dedicated to him in his hometown of Tyana with the blessing of the Roman emperor, Caracalla (188–217 CE). Amulets, supposedly made by Apollonius, were said to protect against a range of problems. Unfortunately, we know little else about the religious milieus that presumably existed around the historical Apollonius, or about the religious veneration directed toward him in the Greco-Roman world. In the manner of religious preachers of his time, he presumably had devotees following him wherever he went, but it is difficult to base any conclusions on the meager data. What we do have extensively documented is the reception history of Philostratus's hagiography. The realization that much of that narrative is a fabrication is relatively recent, and his account of the pious, wise, and godlike philosopher from Tyana generated passionate responses from later authors.

We have stressed the striking similarities between the stories about Jesus and Apollonius. This fact was obvious also to readers in antiquity, pagan as well as Christian, who could use this in polemics against each other, each side accusing the other of plagiarism or of supporting the wrong person. We know, of course, that the followers of Jesus prevailed and that all religions other than Christianity were banned by law at the end of the fourth century. But until the final blow was dealt, Apollonius was repeatedly mentioned as an exceptional example of a divinely inspired, perhaps even divine individual. In fact, the afterlife of Apollonius, or rather of the legend crafted around him, does not end with the victory of Christianity. Many centuries later, when the cultural and political dominance of the Christian churches had weakened sufficiently, there was a renewed interest in Apollonius of Tyana, and, via Philostratus's narrative, he became an icon of pagan wisdom for occultists and other religious dissenters. In one of the more spectacular episodes of this later reception history, the founding figure of French occultism, Eliphas Lévi (1810–75), summoned the spirit of the long-deceased philosopher by means of ritual invocations.

Simon Magus (First Century CE)

The Acts of the Apostles, a text written around 80–90 CE, gives an account of how the earliest followers of Jesus spread the new religion. One of the passages (8:9–23) tells the story of a Samaritan by the name of Simon.[30] The account begins by identifying him as an important religious figure among his own people. He was, according to the anonymous author of Acts, a magician (whence the appellation Magus) and a person whose followers considered him "the power of God." As the tale proceeds, we learn Simon had converted and joined the Jesus movement:

> Now a certain man named Simon had previously practiced magic in the city and amazed the people of Samaria, saying that he was someone great. All of them, from the least to the greatest, listened to him eagerly, saying, "This man is the power of God that is called Great." And they listened eagerly to him because for a long time he had amazed them with his magic. But when they believed Philip, who was proclaiming the good news about the kingdom of God and the name of Jesus Christ, they were baptized, both men and women. Even Simon himself believed. After being baptized, he stayed constantly with Philip and was amazed when he saw the signs and great miracles that took place. (Acts 8:9–13)

The text then states that two of the apostles, John and Peter, traveled to the recently established Samaritan congregation so its members "could receive the Holy Spirit" through the laying on of hands. The narrative continues with a section that describes Simon's inappropriate reaction and Peter's denunciation of Simon:

> Now when Simon saw that the Spirit was given through the laying on of the apostles' hands, he offered them money, saying, "Give me also this power so that anyone on whom I lay my hands may receive the Holy Spirit." But Peter said to him, "May your silver perish with you, because you thought you could obtain God's gift with money! You have no part or share in this, for your heart is not right before God. Repent therefore of this wickedness of yours, and pray to the Lord that, if possible, the intent of your heart may be forgiven you. For I see that you are in the gall of bitterness and the chains of wickedness. (Acts 8:18–23)

The issue at stake is framed in moral terms, but the narrative also reflects how the new religion to which Peter belongs draws boundaries: Simon had previously led his own movement, had despite his conversion retained his erroneous ways, and was swiftly rebuked by the apostle.

---

[30] For a useful summary of scholarship on the shadowy figure of Simon Magus and on the heresiological accounts of him and the movement named after him, see van den Broek 2005.

After the brief account in Acts, the descriptions we have of him and of his teachings come from much later, hostile Christian sources, making the historical Simon Magus exceedingly difficult, perhaps even impossible, to reconstruct. The earliest of these heresiological writers is Justin Martyr (ca. 100–65 CE), who mentions Simon in his *First Apology*, a text written circa 156 CE and addressed to the emperor Antoninus Pius (86–161 CE). Justin claims that many considered Simon a deity and (by misinterpreting a dedication to an ancient Roman deity, Semo Sancus) that the Roman authorities even officially acknowledged his divinity in an inscription on a statue of him:

> There was a Samaritan, Simon, a native of the village called Gitto, who in the reign of Claudius Caesar, and in your royal city of Rome, did mighty acts of magic, by virtue of the art of the devils operating in him. He was considered a god, and as a god was honoured by you with a statue, which statue was erected on the river Tiber, between the two bridges, and bore this inscription, in the language of Rome:

> "Simoni Deo Sancto."
> "To Simon the holy God." (Justin, *First Apology*, 26)

Justin writes that Simon had a close disciple, a former prostitute by the name of Helena, who was "the first idea generated by him." We are also told about his disciple Menander, who proclaimed adherents of their movement would never die. Further details are added in later heresiological accounts. Writing around 180 CE, Irenaeus (ca. 125–202 CE) summarizes the cosmological model Simon is said to have preached (*Against Heresies*, I, 23, 3). The account resembles the basic structure of many Gnostic myths: there are spiritual emanations in several descending layers and, at the lowest level, a feminine emanation, Ennoia, was trapped in a human body and reincarnated over the ages until it had manifested itself in the person of Helena. A text from the early third century, Hippolytus's (d. 235 CE) *Refutation of All Heresies* (VI, sections 2 and 4–15), presents a summary of Simon's teachings that adds considerably more detail and complexity to previous descriptions and states that much of this presentation comes from a text entitled the *Great Revelation* that Simon had allegedly written.

The accounts given by these writers suggest Simon was a historical figure, a person who, like many others in his time, was considered divine by his followers. Facts about him are difficult to separate from legendary materials even in the earliest account. Acts presents him as a convert to Christianity, a statement that may be based on historical fact, but the story of his confrontation with John and Peter is generally understood as a narrative with no historical basis that was constructed in order to make an ideological point. His doctrines have reached us through the polemical presentation of writers whose purpose for summarizing them was to attack them. The fact that later authors add a wealth of details that earlier heresiologists do not mention may be a sign that the concepts the Simonians promulgated were only distantly related to whatever Simon Magus's own teachings may have been. Scholars have sifted through the sources and remain divided over even such basic questions as what the relationship was between the Simonian community and the person of Simon Magus and to what extent the teachings of the Simonians are best categorized as Gnostic (a term that itself has come under intense criticism for encompassing very different traditions).

For the Christian authors who wrote virulent refutations of Simon Magus and his devotees, Simon was a purveyor of a false and devilish message and a competitor to the apostles, who were the rightful heirs of the divine authority that stemmed from Jesus. Irenaeus serves as an example of how this ideological agenda can impact the reading of earlier accounts. The story in Acts frames him as a convert, albeit a flawed one, and the passage even ends with a repentant Simon asking his interlocutor to pray for him (Acts 8:24). Irenaeus, writing a century later, constructs a biography that depicts him in a more sinister light. Simon Magus has now become a person who merely "feigned faith" and after spending some time with the apostles, "applied himself with still greater zeal to the study of the whole magic art, that he might the better bewilder and overpower multitudes of men" (Irenaeus, *Against Heresies* I, 23.1). Narratively framing the Magus as a fake Jesus, Hippolytus contends Simon had his disciples bury him in a trench after claiming that he would arise on the third day, and laconically concludes "he remained (in that grave) until this day, for he was not the Christ" (Hippolytus, *Refutation of All Heresies*, VI, 15). If the historical Apollonius of Tyana remains an elusive figure because the historical facts about him are buried under a mass of hagiographic embellishments, Simon Magus represents the opposite case of a person whose biography is shrouded by vitriolic polemics.

Alexander of Abonoteichus (ca. 105–70 CE)

The scurrilous stories told about Alexander of Abonoteichus (ca. 105–70 CE) are strikingly similar to present-day narratives about the founders of so-called deviant religions offered by anticult organizations (cf. Shupe and Bromley 1994). In fact, nothing seems to have changed fundamentally over the past 2,000 years. New religions tend to evoke hostility and allegations about their nefarious activities. In all likelihood, then as today, there will be a kernel of truth in the accusations, but we should also expect reports by hostile outsiders to contain exaggerations and complete fabrications. Our primary source concerning the life and work of Alexander, a text written by Lucian of Samosata (ca. 120–80 CE), has precisely these characteristics. Lucian is known for works that cast ridicule on a vast range of topics, in particular what he saw as superstitious and naïve forms of religion. His objective in the work that is relevant in the present context is to unmask the protagonist of his narrative as a complete fraud, hence the title *Alexander the False Prophet*. As the name and the genre suggest, we need to proceed cautiously in order to assess the historical facts behind Lucian's satire.[31]

Lucian's plot is constructed around the many lies and manipulations that Alexander allegedly was behind, and we are left with the impression that he was a charming man but an utter charlatan. Lucian writes:

> In sum, imagine, please, and mentally configure a highly diversified soul-blend, made up of lying, trickery, perjury, and malice; facile, audacious, venturesome, diligent in the execution of its schemes, plausible, convincing, masking as good, and wearing an appearance absolutely opposite to its purpose. Indeed, there is nobody who, after meeting him for the first time, did not come away with the idea that he was the most honest and upright man in the world – yes, and the most simple and unaffected. And on top of all this, he had the quality of magnificence, of forming no petty designs but always keeping his mind upon the most important objects. (Lucian, *Alexander the False Prophet*, 4)

Lucian also tells us that in his youth, Alexander was influenced by another dubious con man who was a follower of "the notorious Apollonius," whom we have already met, and adds: "You see what sort of school the man that I am describing comes from!" (Lucian, *Alexander the False Prophet*, 5). We should bear in mind, however, that Lucian was a rationalist who was generally very critically inclined toward many aspects of contemporary religion, oracles in particular, and that his point of view was that of an intellectual. To Alexander's followers, things no doubt looked very different, and the sheer fact that the cult he invented outlived him for more than a century, perhaps even surviving into the fourth century, shows it had a genuine popular appeal. A religious system may work very well even if its founder is dishonest. All it takes is the devotees' trust, and apparently Alexander enjoyed precisely that.

The central object of veneration of Alexander's new religion was a divine, human-headed snake called Glycon. Serpents played a role in many religious contexts, and throughout the area where the cult spread, snakes were seen as

---

[31] Perhaps unsurprisingly, scholarship on Alexander of Abonoteichus has viewed the evidentiary value of Lucian's account in very diverse ways, from seeing it as a work of fiction with only the most tenuous connection to the historical Alexander, to accepting it as a mockingly phrased narrative that nonetheless builds on a substantial factual foundation. Lesgourgues 2018 provides a survey of the literature and assesses how a middle way can be found between these positions.

fertility symbols. Asclepius, the god of medicine and healing, was the best-known deity associated with snakes, and Alexander claimed Glycon, the new god, was in fact an incarnation of Asclepius. According to Lucian, Alexander had at an early stage in his religious career worked with an accomplice. Together, they went to the temple to Apollo in Chalcedon, where they hid engraved bronze tablets announcing Apollo and his son Asclepius would soon leave the temple and take up residence in Abonoteichus, Alexander's home-town. The tablets were conveniently discovered, and people in Abonoteichus began preparing for the divinities' arrival. Alexander, says Lucian, also faked a number of oracles in order to frame himself as divine. Well in advance of this, he had bought a tame snake, which he kept hidden at home. The narrative relates that Alexander:

> prepared and fitted up a serpent's head of linen, which had something of a human look, was all painted up, and appeared very lifelike. It would open and close its mouth by means of horsehairs, and a forked black tongue like a snake's, also controlled by horsehairs, would dart out ... the serpent ... was ready in advance and was being cared for at home, destined in due time to manifest himself to them and to take a part in their show – in fact, to be cast for the leading role. (Lucian, *Alexander the False Prophet*, 12)

So Glycon was introduced. Alexander cut open a goose egg and brought forth a small snake that he declared was the new incarnation of Asclepius. As the story goes, the snake not only grew to the size of a man in less than a week, but, most remarkably, it had the head or face of a human being with long, blond hair.

At this point, a new mythology was in place, a cult image had been produced, and rituals were being prepared. From what we are told, the theology and practices of Alexander's new religion were quite concrete. The god resided in the temple and was readily accessible to those who came for his blessing or advice. Traditionally, religions centered around snakes would focus on fertility and healing, but it seems the cult of Glycon addressed a broader range of issues, which may have stimulated public interest. The practices associated with the cult, however, may provide a better explanation for its success. People had immediate access to Glycon, a living god who would answer their questions directly. Lucian explains that what actually happened was that Alexander himself, with his pet snake adorned with a fake human head coiled around him, would answer people's questions in exchange for a fixed sum of money. Only later, as the new religion became institutionalized and entered the second phase of its existence, was Glycon transformed into a more distant divinity or perhaps even a divine principle, and effigies of snakes with strange heads became ritual objects.

Around 160 CE, the governor of Asia, Publius Mummius Sisenna Rutilianus, publicly defended and promoted the new religion, and even the emperor Marcus Aurelius (121–80 CE) is thought to have consulted the divine oracle. Alexander's Glycon did not develop into an all-important or dominant god within the multireligious landscape of its time, but the new religion found its place in the Hellenistic-Roman polytheistic system and was, for a while, very popular.

The Glycon cult follows a typical pattern for the emergence of new religions: it builds on older traditions, adapts to meet specific demands, offers potential devotees new and striking experiences, and is – at least initially – spearheaded by a charismatic individual. The case also highlights the fact that religions are not necessarily built entirely on honesty and good intentions. What is important, however, is that the religious system works in the sense that it offers something that a sufficient number of people find attractive. Intellectual or moral sophistication is no prerequisite for success. Sometimes religions thrive by being very concrete and tangible. The Glycon cult was still in existence in the third century CE but ultimately disappeared for reasons that, due to the lack of sources, remain unclear.

Charismatic individuals have continued to play major roles in promoting novel religious concepts and practices, and just as in the periods we survey in this Element, they tend to get portrayed in texts that are strongly colored by the perspectives of their authors.[32] Contemporary religious leaders are portrayed as exalted beings in hagiographic narratives penned by their devotees and derided as scoundrels or lunatics by their most vociferous critics. As our examples from antiquity attest, historical facts are merely raw materials that can be combined with legendary accretions in order to produce such ideological narratives. In the absence of such fixtures of the modern world as balanced reporting, the historical Simon Magus or Apollonius of Tyana will presumably never emerge from the sources. As demonstrated by the revival of interest in the latter in occultist milieus, the sheer fact that such sources exist can lead new generations of readers to project their own innovative ideas onto the literary personae of such individuals.

4 Conflict, Concord, and Religious Polemics

In this final section, we will examine some of the ways in which criticism could be leveled against various forms of religion in antiquity. In the contemporary age, the acceptance of various religious options depends on such factors as the

---

[32] There is a quite substantial literature on charismatic leaders of new religions and the textual genres that describe them. For a survey of the issues involved and references to earlier studies, see Rothstein 2016.

details of various national legislation, media responses, the influence of public intellectuals, the role played by representatives of a religious majority, and what can somewhat diffusely be described as popular sentiment. New religious movements differ from each other in innumerable ways, and a common perspective especially in the scholarly literature devoted to them is that a key common trait is their high level of tension with their host societies (Melton 2004; cf. also Lewis and Petersen 2014). A controversial new religion can come into conflict with the law, be disparaged by secular critics for its strange and irrational beliefs and by Christians for deviating from the more recognizable and hence from their perspective more acceptable doctrines of Christianity, be portrayed as a dangerous cult in newspaper reports, and be regarded with suspicion by many in the public at large. Some new religious movements contribute to that tension by being just as vocally critical of mainstream cultural values and of the majority religions of their host societies. Since discourses regarding the boundary between acceptable and unacceptable religion involve many different institutions and individuals with different interests, the situation of any given religion can be quite muddied and messy. In the twenty-first century, for instance, the Church of Scientology is, on one hand, presented by the organization itself as a bona fide religion, based on the insights of a brilliant genius, the movement's founder L. Ron Hubbard (1911–86), and boasts of the support of celebrities such as actor Tom Cruise.[33] On the other hand, the organization and the beliefs and practices it promotes have been portrayed in extremely negative terms in documentaries such as *Going Clear* and *My Scientology Movie* and have been criticized in countless books. Its legal status as a religion varies from country to country. It is accepted as such in the United States, Switzerland, and Sweden, for example, whereas countries such as France, Belgium, Germany, and Russia have not granted it that status and have met the organization with various degrees of hostility.[34]

Boundaries were also drawn between acceptable and unacceptable religions in antiquity, and the details were no less messy then. Focusing on the Roman period, we will in this section briefly present examples of ways in which such boundary work was carried out, not only against religions that were new at the time but against unacceptable religion generally, noting differences and similarities with modern equivalents along the way. Counterparts of present-day secular critics of religion were rare in Roman antiquity, but we will begin by briefly presenting examples of such broadly aimed appraisals. A far more prevalent tendency was to

---

[33] For a closer examination of how Hubbard is venerated, see Refslund Christensen 2005 and Rothstein 2017.

[34] The literature on the legal status of Scientology includes Palmer 2009, Richardson 2009, and Carobene 2014.

consider a particular religion or type of religious practice acceptable and others unacceptable: the religions of other peoples, considered barbarians; those practiced in Rome but characterized by some writers as unsuitable for Romans; practices subsumed under the label "magic"; and Christianity and Manichaeism, religions viewed with varying degrees of hostility. We end this section by briefly considering the polemics engaged in by Christian apologists who argued religions other than their own should be condemned.

Antireligious Polemics

In the modern period, a broadly aimed criticism against religion is associated with philosophers such as Baruch Spinoza in the seventeenth century and David Hume in the eighteenth, and is later taken up by innumerable others who fight against what they describe as the irrationality and deleterious nature of religion. Public intellectuals such as Richard Dawkins and the late Christopher Hitchens would be just two contemporary examples. This form of criticism typically follows lines of reasoning that suggest the following: that religion constitutes the attempt by people who did not know any better to explain the workings of the natural world; that it builds on psychological mechanisms such as fear and hope; and that it becomes a tool in the hands of the ruling strata of society. As the last of these arguments suggests, criticism of religion in general is often used to specifically condemn the dominant religion of the society in which the thinker in question lives rather than as a weapon directed at minorities. Spinoza's Jewish background and Hume's place in a society dominated by Christianity colored their antireligious arguments.

Similarly argued critiques against religion in general on rationalist grounds are uncommon in texts from antiquity.[35] An example is Lucretius's (ca. 99–55 BCE) didactic poem *De rerum natura*. Although the text presents significant interpretive difficulties, the author does not seem to have denied the existence of the gods. In his view, however, they have not created the cosmos and play no role in human affairs. They function mainly as role models: just as the gods are to be thought of as completely unmoved by us and our affairs, we should also strive for complete inner composure. Traditional forms of religious worship are, from this perspective, not meaningful:

> It is no piety to show oneself often with covered head, turning towards a stone and approaching every altar, none to fall prostrate upon the ground and to spread open the palms before shrines of the gods, none to sprinkle altars with the blood of beasts in showers and to link vow to vow; but rather to be able to survey all things with peace at mind. (Lucretius, *De rerum natura* 5, 1198–1203)

---

[35] On antireligious critiques in antiquity, see Bremmer 2007.

The reason most people believe the gods do play an active role in human affairs is, in Lucretius's view, not least their futile attempt to explain natural phenomena:

> They observed how the array of heaven and the various seasons of the year came round in due order and could not discover by what causes all that came about. Therefore their refuge was to leave all in the hands of the gods, and to suppose that by their nod all things were done. And they placed the gods' abode and habitation in the sky, because through the sky the moon and the night are seen to revolve, moon and day and night and the solemn stars of night, heaven's light-wandering torches, clouds and sun, rain and snow, winds, lightnings and hail, rapid roarings and threatening throes of thunder. (Lucretius, *De rerum natura* 5, 1183–94)

Other texts can be interpreted as skeptical criticisms against specific features in established forms of Roman religion. Cicero's (106–43 BCE) *On Divination*, written in 45–44 BCE, is set as a dialogue between his brother Quintus and himself, in which the former presents arguments for divination, a central part of official Roman religion, and Cicero (or rather his literary persona) proceeds to demolish those arguments and discredit the practice. Why, he asks, would such utterly different events as detecting a particular detail in the appearance of a liver and financial gain have anything to do with each other (2, 34)? Why are omens so dark and enigmatic that they are open to the most diverse interpretations (2, 132)? Why are there conflicting systems of interpretation of the same omens among soothsayers from different cultures (2, 28)? Surely, if the gods wanted to communicate their will, they would have chosen more adequate ways of doing so.

Acceptable and Unacceptable Religion

Although rejections of religion, or of entire sectors of religious practice, seem to have been uncommon, distinctions were commonly made between the right way of worshipping the gods (often labeled *religio*) and the wrong way (*superstitio*).[36] The dichotomy owed much to Greek ideas about the difference between true piety and *deisidaimonia*, a term deployed to designate practices that in the eyes of various authors were excessive or inappropriate. In the Latin-speaking world, the terms *religio* and *superstitio* started out as neutral terms but soon acquired the normative connotations the corresponding labels had in much Greek philosophical thinking. A variety of reasons could be offered for distinguishing between them. In *The Nature of the Gods* (1, 117), Cicero explains a distinction can be drawn between the groundless fear of the gods (*superstitio*) and the pious worship of them (*religio*). The difference here seems not to be the substance

---

[36] Our brief summary is primarily based on Martin 2004.

of the religious practice (i.e., which gods are involved or what the purpose of the ritual may be), but the attitude of the individual carrying out the ritual. In his *Pro Cluentio* (68, 194), however, *superstitio* is the use of religious means to cause harm. Here, Cicero rhetorically distinguishes "the favour of Heaven . . . gained by duty done to God and man" from "base superstition and victims offered for the success of crime." In his thirteenth *Satire*, Juvenal (ca. 55–135 CE) lampoons a man who, outraged at a petty offense, takes recourse in the gods. Here, the wrong way to be religious is to lack balance and moderation by assuming the deities would intervene in the trivial personal problems of a particular individual. As expressed by classicist James Uden, beyond satirizing the behavior of one man, a picture is painted of a world of excessive religion,

> a world where adulterous liaisons take place at shrines of Isis, Peace, Cybele, and Ceres; where the Roman consular Lateranus swears by the Gallic horse god Epona at the altars of Jove; where the satirist himself can casually invoke details of Egyptian cult while lamenting the disappearance of Roman *virtus*. The *Satires* do not insist emphatically on the worship of any particular god. They depict an Empire in which the old gods have become part of a crowd. (Uden 2019: 101; footnotes in the original have been removed)

Although the reasons for setting boundaries can seem shifting and vague (how much religion is too much?), the line between acceptable and unacceptable religion was often drawn against practices that could undermine the social order. The historian Livy (59 BCE–17 CE) gives an exposé of the so-called Bacchanalian Affair that took place in Rome in the year 186 BCE (*History of Rome*, 39, 8–19). A newly introduced cult devoted to Bacchus, also known as Dionysus, was considered a public danger and forcefully suppressed. Accusations of all kinds were filed against the movement: participants were said to indulge in illicit sex, drunkenness, murder, deceit, and immorality of every kind. However, as Morten Warmind (1999: 56–7) noted, it seems the real concern was the fact that freeborn Romans mingled with slaves in a religious fellowship that bound them together in solidarity. It was thus not the religious beliefs as such nor the ritual acts of the Bacchanalian religion that caused alarm but the cult's threat to the social order. Livy himself does not accuse the cult itself of being a false religion, even if he portrays the anonymous instigator of the whole thing as a morally corrupt individual.

Negative Attitudes toward Magic

Among the practices most frowned upon in Rome – far more than in ancient Greece, if the works of the literate elite and recorded legislation are to be taken as accurate representations of social attitudes – were those branded as magic (or other terms that over the course of Roman religious history were conflated with magic).[37] The term *magia* is not attested in Latin earlier than the first century BCE and is from its inception associated with practices that are of foreign origin and are to varying degrees seen as in opposition to the established religious customs of Rome.[38] An example of how magic could be conceptualized as a set of grotesque and immoral activities is Horace's (65–8 BCE) *Fifth Epode*, a poem written circa 30 BCE, in which a witch by the name of Canidia manufactures a love potion from the bone marrow and liver of a boy. The concept soon became assimilated with earlier ideas about maleficent rituals. *The Laws of the Twelve Tables*, an ancient set of laws dating back to the fifth century BCE, prescribes harsh punishments for people who harm others or steal the crops from their fields by means of songs. A law directed against poisoners and assassins, *Lex cornelia de sicariis et veneficis* (the Cornelian Law against Murderers and Poisoners), was adopted in 81 BCE. Both were retroactively interpreted to deal also with cases involving people who carried out magical rituals.

Besides texts that portray magic as evil, a second mode of attack is to portray magic as deceptive and useless and those who dabble in such practices as deluded. An example of an author who pursues this line of attack is Pliny the Elder (23–79 CE), who devotes substantial space in his *Natural History* to what he calls "the most fraudulent of arts" (Pliny, *Natural History*, 30, 1). In Pliny's account, magic is a heterodox category of foreign – that is, non-Roman – practices, a cultural stage that Rome has passed but of which traces can be found in very early sources. Among the practices he includes as examples of magic are attempts to cure various ailments with remedies made of animal products or involving contact with animals. Pliny writes in a tone of utter derision that magicians consider moles in particular to have extraordinary powers (*Natural History* 30, 7).[39] After a number of such recipes Pliny describes as the foolish methods employed by magicians, the list of remedies continues in a much more neutral tone, and nothing substantial seems to differentiate cures based on magic from cures Pliny seemingly endorses. The

---

[37] We should perhaps clarify that we are here not concerned with practices that might be considered "magic" under various scholarly definitions of the contested term, but with the drawing of boundaries against practices understood as constituting magic that one finds in Roman sources.

[38] Interestingly, analogous dichotomies still apply to widespread Western perceptions of "our" religious ways compared to the magic and superstition of "others."

[39] Pliny does not explain why magicians think of these animals as particularly powerful but ridicules these seemingly deluded people who attribute a special potency to what he describes as a rather pathetic animal that is blind and doomed to live underground. It is tempting to see their fascination with moles, as cultural anthropologist Mary Douglas might have done, as precisely a consequence of the remarkable liminal nature of these creatures who inhabit the borderland between this world and a subterranean realm.

contention that magic is illusory and the apparent difficulty in even demarcating a separate field of magic in the first place do not prevent Pliny from seeing it as a barbaric custom that should be stamped out. The druids make an appearance in this context, since their suppression under Emperor Tiberius (42 BCE–37 CE) is portrayed as an example of how the Romans managed to end various "monstrous rites" (Pliny, *Natural History*, 30, 4).

The two understandings – magic as evil and as nonsense – also coalesce in the earliest record of a trial against a person accused of magic, the *Apology* or *Apologia sive pro se de magia* written by Apuleius of Madaura.[40] Apuleius had married a wealthy widow by the name of Pudentilla, and her disgruntled relatives charged him with having resorted to magic in his attempts to get her to agree to the arrangement. A trial was held, probably in 158 or 159 CE, and Apuleius successfully defended himself. Since he was put on trial for his actions, legislation must have been invoked that regarded the practice of magic as a punishable offense. His *Apologia*, however, consists less of a legal defense against the charge of having performed magic than of an argument that the very concept of magic as understood by his adversaries was incoherent and absurd. Apuleius summarizes the various activities that were purportedly examples of magic, and these do come across as a rather random set of events: the accused had bought fish for supposedly maleficent purposes, had been present when a boy inexplicably fell to the ground, and had stored an unknown object in a linen cloth. The Roman conception of magic comes across here as a term that could be used ad hoc as an allegation against people with whom one had conflicts.

Controversies over Foreign Practices

As we have repeatedly seen, the borders of Roman religion were porous, and over Rome's long history, numerous foreign deities were incorporated and new religious practices emerged that to varying degrees were accepted. Controversies did, however, arise with the core issue typically being the extent to which a religious practice could pose a menace to the public order (Margel 2006: 195). Negative reactions against these religions ranged on a spectrum from rhetorical diatribes to repressive measures.

The cult of Cybele or Mother Goddess shows how ambivalent attitudes toward religious imports could be. As we have already seen, devotion to Cybele met with a mixed reception, since it was associated with some practices that seemed appropriate to Roman mores and others that were reviled as outlandish and repugnant. Ovid, in his *Fasti* (IV, 175–372), relates legends

---

[40] Otto 2011: 235–64 presents the details.

that, on one hand, made the cult seem radically alien and, on the other hand, provided an explanation for why a goddess imported from Phrygia (cf. Section 1) had actually been a Roman deity from the very beginning. The Romans, the legend goes, could trace their roots to the homeland of the goddess, and when their ancestor Aeneas left Troy for the Italian peninsula, she almost decided to follow him but ultimately remained behind. Five centuries later, the time was ripe, and a Roman expedition was sent to Phrygia. The local king, Attalus, at first refused, but when the goddess herself insisted she wished to go to Rome, the terrified monarch did not dare oppose her. In this way, a deity that according to a well-known myth had driven her first devotee, Attis, to madness and, in an utterly un-Roman act, inspired him to emasculate himself, could nonetheless be installed in the city as a goddess with a deep connection to the Roman people.

The distinction between a good Roman mode of venerating the goddess and a bad foreign way comes across with particular clarity in the following passage, where the Greek historian Dionysius of Halicarnassus (ca. 60–7 BCE) describes her worship:

> [T]he praetors perform sacrifices and celebrate games in her honour every year according to the Roman customs, but a Phrygian man and a Phrygian woman act as her priests, and it is they who carry her image in procession through the city, begging alms in her name according to their custom, and wearing figures upon their breasts and striking their timbrels while their followers play tunes upon their flutes in honour of the Mother of the Gods. But by a law and decree of the senate no native Roman walks in procession through the city arrayed in a parti-coloured robe, begging alms or escorted by flute-players, or worships the god with the Phrygian ceremonies. (Dionysius of Halicarnassus, *Roman Antiquities* II.19, 4–5)

The din and clamor of the Phrygians and the gaudy outfits they wear are, at least according to Dionysius, utterly inappropriate for true Romans, even though the goddess is celebrated on the streets of the city. The deity is deemed worthy of devotion, but a boundary that is social rather than theological is drawn against rituals that go against the norms of correct Roman behavior.

Support by the elite could give a religious practice needed legitimacy. The Roman cult of Isis is an apt illustration of this phenomenon.[41] The originally Egyptian goddess took hold in the Hellenized eastern Mediterranean by the middle of the third century BCE and, with increasing Roman dominance over the region, reached Rome in the last century BCE. A priesthood of the goddess was established in Rome by the late 80s BCE (Bricault 2013: 178). As part of its

---

[41] The social transformation of the cult of Isis is usefully presented in Bøgh 2013; the present summary is largely dependent on that study.

transfer out of an Egyptian setting, devotion to Isis took on the characteristics of a mystery religion. Since the cult of Isis was considered foreign, devotion to her was at first controversial. On one hand, one of the most powerful men in the city, the *pontifex maximus* and consul Quintus Caecilius Metellus Pius (128–63 BCE), seems to have founded a temple to the deity. On the other hand, other segments of the political elite fought the introduction of the new practices, and in the 50s and 40s BCE, and again in the 20s, temples and altars dedicated to Isis were destroyed.[42] Gradually, the worship of Isis gained the acceptance of the upper classes and five days were devoted to a festival celebrating the goddess. Under the reign of Caligula, who had a temple to the goddess built in the year 38 CE, the cult was backed by the most powerful man in the Roman Empire. Successive emperors had varying degrees of interest in the Isiac mystery religion, ranging from a modest degree of endorsement to enthusiastic support. Only with the rise to power of Christianity in the fourth century did the veneration of Isis once again meet with repression. A final stronghold in the periphery of the empire, the temple at Philae near present-day Aswan in southern Egypt, was closed by force by order of the Byzantine emperor Justinian I (482–565 CE) in 536 CE.[43]

Religions of Barbaric Foreigners

Despite the general inclusivity of the Roman religious landscape, there are examples of attempts by the authorities to quash religions deemed a direct threat to Rome. The increasingly harsh measures taken against the religious practices of the Gauls is a case in point. The most detailed description of Gallic religion is found in *The Gallic War*, Caesar's account of his war of conquest of their land, waged from 58 to 50 BCE. Inserted into his chronicle of military campaigns are passages devoted to the way of life of the peoples he encountered, including the religion of Gaul and the place of its priesthood, the druids, in Gallic society.[44] Much of Caesar's book on the Gallic war is a seemingly unadorned chrono-logical narrative of the subjugation of various Celtic tribes, and the matter-of-fact tone can give the impression that Caesar is simply retelling some basic facts about their religion. However, one needs to keep in mind when reading the book in general, and the description of the druids in particular, that Caesar had a vested interest in presenting the conquest of Gaul and his own role in the

---

[42] The extent of these persecutions was connected with the intensity of the political conflicts between Rome and Egypt; compare Bøgh 2013.

[43] The history of the Isis mystery religion in Rome is summarized in Heyob 1975: 1–36 and Bøgh 2013. The contentious question of a link between the veneration of Isis and the Christian cult of Mary is usefully surveyed in McGuckin 2008 and Higgins 2012.

[44] *The Gallic War* 6, 13; 6, 14; 6, 16–18.

events in a positive light, and that his story is narrated in a carefully curated fashion.

Gallic society is presented as very hierarchical and organized in such a way that two classes at the highest level wield almost absolute power: the *equites* and the *druides*. The former, a warrior class, need not concern us further. The functions of the druids, as Caesar describes them, were numerous and diverse. They were diviners, priests, and judges. They were repositories of a vast and complex storehouse of orally transmitted knowledge that took twenty years to fully master. The prestige of being a druid was such that many young men took upon themselves the onerous task of going through the lengthy course of education. They taught some form of afterlife belief according to which the soul passes from one body to another, which may either be a way of describing transmigration or a concept of a realm beyond death resembling our own world to which the soul passes. Caesar furthermore describes them as learned men preoccupied with "the stars and their movement, the size of the cosmos and the earth, the world of nature, the power of deities." All of these qualities can be construed as positive or at least neutral, but the following passage paints the druids in a quite different light:

> The whole nation of the Gauls is greatly devoted to ritual observances, and for that reason those who are smitten with the more grievous maladies and who are engaged in the perils of battle either sacrifice human victims or vow so to do, employing the druids as ministers for such sacrifices. They believe, in effect, that, unless for a man's life a man's life be paid, the majesty of the immortal gods may not be appeased; and in public, as in private, life they observe an ordinance of sacrifices of the same kind. Others use figures of immense size, whose limbs, woven out of twigs, they fill with living men and set on fire, and the men perish in a sheet of flame. (Caesar, *The Gallic War*, 6, 16)

Archaeological evidence suggests human sacrifice did take place, though the description of these violent rituals in Caesar's text should be seen within the context of portraying Rome as embarked on a civilizing mission to include putatively barbarian nations within its territory.[45]

The description of the druids as a group with great power over Gallic society explains why the Roman authorities took measures to curb their influence. Augustus forbade Roman citizens from participating in druidic rituals. Claudius went a step further and in 41 CE outlawed druidic practices. Tacitus

---

[45] See Rose 2019 for a thorough analysis of the archaeological evidence. A section on the relationship between these material remains and the literary source is utterly dismissive of the documentary value of the latter (Rose 2019: 212–18). See also Hutton (2009: 1–48) for a systematic and equally critical review of the literary sources.

(*Annals* 14, 30) relates that under Emperor Nero (37–68 CE), a large group of druids in Britain were massacred and their groves destroyed. These measures were by Roman standards quite extreme. Generally, the beliefs and practices connected with the Gallic polytheistic pantheon seems to have been of little concern to the Romans. The case of the druids should largely be seen as Roman politics directed against a group of people the state regarded as a dangerous source of anti-Roman sentiment.

Polemics and Persecution in the Early History of Christianity

Among the various forms of religion Roman sources depict in a particularly negative light one finds Christianity. Roman literati described the new religion during the first three centuries of its existence as a gross form of *superstitio*. If we are to believe Christian writers of this period who defended their religion, Christians were accused of engaging in immoral sexual behavior, even of cannibalism.[46] Christians, it was rumored, held wild orgies: according to this tall tale, a dog was tied to a lamp and made to overturn the only source of light in the room where men, women, and children were assembled. In the ensuing darkness everybody proceeded to have indiscriminate sex.

Popular resentment and prejudice against the Christians are documented not only in such texts. A graffito from the city of Rome, dated to circa 200 CE, shows a man in front of a crucified, donkey-headed human figure, accompanied by the words *Alexamenos sebete theon*, "Alexamenos worships [his] god." We know from various sources there was a widespread rumor that the Christians worshipped a deity with the head of a donkey. Tertullian, for instance, devotes a lengthy section of his *Apology* (ch. 16) to presenting and rebutting the claim. The crude graffito also uses other visual elements that make it clear Christians are targeted. Apart from the most obvious clue, the cross, the crucified man in the graffito is depicted as wearing a *perizoma*, a type of loincloth that would become a standard iconographic element in later images of Jesus on the cross. In fact, victims of Roman crucifixion were naked, but the artist knew exactly what to draw in order to mock Alexamenos for his adherence to Christianity.[47]

Christians were not only the object of polemics and ridicule: at least periodically they were actively persecuted.[48] Considering the amount of research devoted to the issue, it is quite remarkable that there is considerable disagreement about how intense and systematic this persecution was. Historians of the period have concluded there is little evidence that there was any hostility

---

[46] These lurid accusations are usefully presented in Wagemakers 2010.

[47] On the Alexamenos graffito, see Harley-McGowan 2020.

[48] A seminal article on this topic is De Ste. Croix 1963. For a detailed discussion of Roman attitudes toward the Christians, see Cook 2010.

directed at them before the reign of Nero, except by Jews who reacted against what they must have perceived as a heterodox schismatic group within their own community. The first systematic persecution, in the view of most scholars, took place in the year 64 CE under Nero, but even in this case, dissenting voices have noted we have only one single source documenting this event: Tacitus *Annals* 15, 44.[49]

Persecutions remained local and sporadic until the reign of Decius (201–51 CE) in the mid-third century, who was the first emperor to persecute the Christians throughout the empire for their refusal to sacrifice to the Roman gods.[50] Later waves of repression against the Christians took place under Emperor Valerian (ca. 200–60 CE) in 257 to 260 CE, and under Diocletian (236–316 CE). Beginning in 303, Diocletian issued a series of edicts that purged the army of Christians, ordered the arrest of Christian clergy, and ordered Christians to participate in sacrifices or be executed. Anti-Christian polemics may resemble verbal attacks against new religions in our own times, but during periods of persecution, the Roman state engaged in theatrical displays of extreme violence against Christians that have no counterpart in the present age. Like other criminals, they could face crucifixion or being mauled to death by wild animals.

The fact that Christians were targeted for not sacrificing to the emperor's genius is symptomatic of the issues involved: the line was drawn to exclude a group for its putatively anti-Roman behavior, whereas its beliefs seem to have been of little concern. The extent to which Christians were beleaguered also varied greatly over time and, depending on who was the ruler during a particular period, Christians could face death or be left in peace. Persecution finally ended in the western part of the empire after Diocletian resigned in 305, but it continued in the eastern part of the empire under Galerius (250–311 CE) and Maximinus Daza (270–313 CE). Galerius issued an edict to end the hostilities shortly before his death in 311. Two years later, in 313, Maximinus also ended persecution, and Christianity was poised to soon become the main player on the religious arena.

Roman Rejection of the Manichaeans

Less well known outside the ranks of specialists on religion than the Roman persecution of Christians is the fact that the Roman authorities also clamped down on another putative world religion, Manichaeism.[51] The basic tenets of

---

[49] For a dissenting voice, see Shaw 2015.   [50] On the Decian persecution, see Rives 1999.
[51] For the spread of Manichaeism to the Roman Empire, see the extensive discussion in Lieu 1992; on the persecution of Manichaeism by Diocletian, see Lieu 1992: 121–24.

this new religion, created by the prophet Mani, were discussed in Section 2. One characteristic aspect of Manichaeism was its emphasis on missionizing. Mani believed several former prophets, including Zarathustra, Buddha, and Jesus, had revealed the same message as he did, but that their teachings had been corrupted by their followers. Mani's ambition was to transcend geographical, linguistic, and cultural boundaries and bring the true teaching to the entire world. Manichaeism spread rapidly through the Greco-Roman world, arriving in the eastern provinces in the 260s CE, proceeding from there to Egypt and on westward along the Mediterranean coast, and at some point in time reaching the city of Rome itself.[52] Although cults of foreign origin were a well-established part of the religious landscape, the emperor, Diocletian, decided the presence of this religion should not be tolerated in his realm. In 297 CE, he proclaimed an edict against the Manichaeans, several years before the last serious persecution of the Christians in the empire was initiated in 303 CE. To many observers, no doubt, the Christians and the Manichaeans were difficult to distinguish, not least because the Manichaeans also saw Jesus as a prominent figure in their belief system, its founder claimed to be his apostle, and Manichaean texts presented the religion as a form of Christianity. Diocletian nevertheless targeted the two groups independently. The official edict that ordered the persecution of the followers of Mani is very harsh in its condemnation of the new religion:

> We have heard that the Manichaeans ... have set up new and hitherto unheard-of sects in opposition to the older creeds so that they might cast out the doctrines vouchsafed to us in the past by the divine favour for the benefit of their own depraved doctrine. They have sprung forth very recently like new and unexpected monstrosities among the race of the Persians – a nation still hostile to us – and have made their way into our empire, where they are committing many outrages, disturbing the tranquility of our people and even inflicting grave damage to the civic communities. We have cause to fear that with the passage of time they will endeavour, as usually happens, to infect the modest and tranquil of an innocent nature with the damnable customs and perverse laws of the Persians as with the poison of a malignant (serpent) ... We order that the authors and leaders of these sects be subjected to severe punishment, and, together with their abominable writings, burnt in the flames. We direct their followers, if they continue recalcitrant, shall suffer capital punishment, and their goods be forfeited to the imperial treasury. And if those who have gone over to that hitherto unheard-of, scandalous and wholly infamous creed, or to that of the Persians, are persons who hold public office, or are of any rank or of superior social status, you will see to it that their estates are confiscated and the

---

[52] One single source identifies a missionary by the name of Bundos who supposedly brought the new religion to Rome during the reign of Diocletian, but the historical value of this text is open to doubt (Gardner and Lieu 2004: 116–17).

offenders sent to the (quarry) at Phaeno or the mines at Proconnesus. (transl.
in Lieu 1992: 121–22)

The text identifies Manichaeism as a pernicious innovation coming from Persia,
a nation Rome saw as an enemy. The claim is problematic, to say the least, since
Mani was also seen as a threat by the leaders of Persia's state religion,
Zoroastrianism, and was executed in 277 CE. The vitriolic language of the
edict provides few other specific reasons for the emperor's wrath. Certainly,
Mani's cosmology, which saw the world as an evil place, was very different
from the traditional religion of the empire, where the gods were in a sense seen
as stakeholders in the good fortune of Roman society. Perhaps, however, the
reason for adopting such draconian measures against the Manichaeans was
political rather than strictly religious. Diocletian was a conservative ruler who
wished to restore Roman virtues and revive the cult of the divinized emperor,
a self-serving move in that he declared himself the son of Jupiter. Whereas other
rulers in earlier times might have ignored or even welcomed the newcomers,
Diocletian decided the Manichaeans should be met with the utmost brutality.

After the Christianization of the Roman Empire, Manichaeism continued to
be persecuted and ultimately died out there. The religion survived for many
centuries in Central Asia and China, but the last traces of a living Manichaean
community disappeared around 1600.

Drawing Boundaries around an Emerging Christian Orthodoxy

The analogy between the situation of modern new religious movements and that
of minority religions in the Hellenistic and Roman periods ultimately breaks
down in one crucial respect: for the most part, new religious movements in the
contemporary period have remained minority religions.[53] By contrast, in the
late days of the Roman Empire, a single one of the many coexisting religions
was vigorously promoted: Christianity. With the rise to prominence and power
of the new religion came a shift in focus regarding where the borders around
acceptable religion should be drawn. As we have noted, the movers and shakers
of pre-Christian Rome tended to judge religions according to such criteria as the
extent to which they were in accordance with Roman ways of behaving and
whether they might be a threat to political stability. The earliest texts of the new
religion – that is, the authentic letters of Paul – address the quite different issue

---

[53] Note, though, that in some cases, new religious movements have grown to an impressive size and
are, at least regionally, not minority religions. The Church of Jesus Christ of Latter-day Saints
(the "Mormons"), for instance, has 17 million adherents worldwide (https://newsroom.church
ofjesuschrist.org/article/2022-statistical-report-april-2023-conference). In its historical heart-
land, Utah, the Church of Jesus Christ of Latter-day Saints comprises two-thirds of the state's
population (https://newsroom.churchofjesuschrist.org/facts-and-statistics/state/utah).

of whether a religious belief or practice has a divine or demonic origin. The First Epistle to the Corinthians, dated around 53–4 CE, establishes a stark distinction between the ritual celebration of the last supper and the ritual offering of food to idols: "No, I imply that what pagans sacrifice, they sacrifice to demons and not to God. I do not want you to be partners with demons. You cannot drink the cup of the Lord and the cup of demons. You cannot partake of the table of the Lord and the table of demons" (1 Corinthians 10:20–1).

The Second Epistle to the Corinthians, dated 55–6 CE, presents an equally sharp dichotomy between followers of Christ and unbelievers and an exhortation to shun the latter:

> Do not be mismatched with unbelievers. For what partnership is there between righteousness and lawlessness? Or what fellowship is there between light and darkness? What agreement does Christ have with Beliar? Or what does a believer share with an unbeliever? What agreement has the temple of God with idols? For we are the temple of the living God; as God said, "I will live in them and walk among them, and I will be their God, and they shall be my people. Therefore come out from them, and be separate from them, says the Lord, and touch nothing unclean; then I will welcome you, and I will be your father, and you shall be my sons and daughters, says the Lord Almighty." (2 Corinthians 6:4–18)

This insistence on drawing sharp distinctions between true and false religions became a long-lasting motif in the history of Christianity. At first, the form of Christianity that would ultimately emerge victorious was a minority religion with little clout. The borders between acceptable and unacceptable religion were constructed in a discourse of varying polemical intensity rather than in political life. The demarcation between true and demonic is a recurrent one in this substantial literature. Contrary to the often remarkably vague Roman conceptions of what constituted unacceptable religion, Christian sources can go into hairsplitting detail. They do so not least to brand other versions of Christianity than their own as false because of their supposedly faulty understanding of the nature of the figure they all revere: Christ.

Some Christian authors who engaged in verbal battles against their ideological foes could, like Irenaeus of Lyons, focus on other Christian sects. Others, such as Bishop Epiphanius of Salamis (310/20–403 CE), included a broad spectrum of movements in the entire region among their enemies. Since the purpose of this literature is to identify false and demonic religions, the language is often extremely harsh and polemical. For instance, the *Panarion* or Medicine Chest written by Epiphanius is a theologically biased description of eighty different movements, most of which are likened to various dangerous animals. In his discussion of one of the most important competitors to orthodox

Christianity, the Valentinians, Epiphanius writes that they "are in the power of demons" (Epiphanius, *Panarion*, 34.5) and of their founder, Valentinus, he suggests that:

> [B]y sowing his dreaming in many people and calling himself a Gnostic, Valentinus has, as it were, fastened a number of scorpions together in one chain, as in the old and well-known parable. It says that scorpions, one after another, will form a sort of chain to a length of ten or even more, let themselves down from a roof or housetop, and so do their harm to men by guile. (Epiphanius, *Panarion*, 36.4)

After having been ridiculed and recurrently persecuted for nearly three centuries, Christianity in the fourth century CE rapidly transitioned into being tolerated, then privileged, and finally declared the only religion that could be legally practiced. Powerful supporters of Christianity went from verbal attacks to political persecution. In 380 CE, laws were passed (Theodosian Code 16, 1.2) that commanded all subjects of the emperor to profess the Christian religion in one particular theological variant and proclaimed all others were heretics subject to divine condemnation and legal punishment. Waves of repression and campaigns of destruction of pre-Christian religious sites swept the empire numerous times beginning in the 390s.

Concluding Observations

We began our narrative by stressing that cultural imports need to make sense within their new cultural context. Imperial legislation and attempts to impose orthodoxy notwithstanding, the spread of Christianity over vast areas entailed the emergence of local practices and beliefs. Lived religion tends to deal with matters of everyday concern such as tackling adversity, seeking relief from illness, and ensuring good fortune. David Frankfurter discusses these developments in Egypt and documents how people in the early Christian period sought help from holy men, visited local shrines, performed locally crafted rituals, used protective spells and wore amulets, and developed ways of being Christian that seem far removed from any textually based orthodoxy. Religious leaders could be highly critical of some practices but accept others. The late fourth- and early fifth-century abbot and reformer Shenoute of Atripe complained bitterly about the folly of people who poured out libations, burned incense to "phantoms" or slept at shrines in order to receive significant dreams, but supported the display of symbols of the Nile during processions (Frankfurter 2018: 13, 18).

Measures to impose religious uniformity clearly did not mean a religious monoculture, based on the norms and values of a class of religious experts, was ever achieved. Throughout the history of Christianity in all its many forms, shifting attitudes have resulted in a dazzling variety of ways in which elite norms and facts on the ground have coexisted. The religious landscape had by the cusp of the fifth century nevertheless begun to change in fundamental ways. The pre-Christian world took a pluralistic and malleable approach to the suprahuman dimension for granted as long as the social order was not seen as under grave threat. Henceforth, potential deviations from orthodoxy would become a matter of recurring concern and triggered innumerable efforts to enforce discipline.

References

Primary Sources

All New Testament quotations are taken from *The New Oxford Annotated Bible*. 2007. Edited by M. D. Coogan. New York: Oxford University Press.

Other sources from antiquity are quoted from the following editions:

Anonymous Texts

Apocalypse of Peter. In J. K. Elliott, ed. 1924. *The Apocryphal New Testament*. Oxford: Oxford University Press, pp. 593–615.

Gospel of Thomas. In J. K. Elliott, ed. 1924. *The Apocryphal New Testament*. Oxford: Oxford University Press, pp. 123–47.

Homeric Hymn to Demeter. 2018. Translated by G. Nagy. Center for Hellenic Studies, Harvard University. https://archive.chs.harvard.edu/CHS/article/display/5292 (webpage dated February 12, 2018).

Papyri Graecae Magicae = Betz, H. D. 1992. *The Greek Magical Papyri in Translation, including the Demotic Spells. Vol. 1: Texts*. 2nd ed. Chicago, IL: Chicago University Press.

Apuleius

The Golden Ass or Metamorphoses. 2004. Translated with an introduction and notes by E. J. Kenney. Harmondsworth: Penguin.

Augustus

Res Gestae Divi Augusti. 2009. Text, translation, and commentary by A. E. Cooley. Cambridge: Cambridge University Press.

Caesar

The Gallic War. 1917. Translated by H. J. Edwards. Loeb Classical Library. Cambridge, MA: Harvard University Press.

Cicero

Pro Cluentio: *Pro Lege Manilia. Pro Caecina. Pro Cluentio. Pro Rabirio Perduellionis Reo*. 1927. With an English translation by H. Grose Hodge. Loeb Classical Library. Cambridge, MA: Harvard University Press.

Dionysius of Halicarnassus

The Roman Antiquities of Dionysius of Halicarnassus. 1960. With an English translation by E. Cary on the basis of the version of E. Spelman. Loeb Classical Library. London: William Heinemann.

Epiphanius of Salamis

Panarion. The Panarion *of Epiphanius of Salamis: Book 1 (Sects 1–46)*. 2nd ed. 2008. Translated by F. Williams. Leiden: Brill.

Hippolytus of Rome

Refutation of All Heresies. 1886. Translated by J. H. MacMahon. In A. Roberts and J. Donaldson, eds., *The Ante-Nicene Fathers*, Vol. 6. Edinburgh: T&T Clark, pp. 25–403.

Irenaeus of Lyons

Against Heresies. 1885. Translated by A. Roberts and J. Donaldson. In P. Schaff, A. Roberts, and J. Donaldson, eds., *The Ante-Nicene Fathers*, Vol. 1. Edinburgh: T&T Clark, pp. 841–1391.

Justin Martyr

First Apology. 1885. Translated by A. Roberts and J. Donaldson. In P. Schaff, A. Roberts, and J. Donaldson, eds., *The Ante-Nicene Fathers*, Vol. 1. Edinburgh: T&T Clark, pp. 423–97.

Lucian

Alexander the False Prophet: *Lucian*. 1936. With an English translation by A. M. Harmon. 8 vols. Loeb Classical Library. London: William Heinemann, vol. 4, pp. 173–253.

Lucretius

De rerum natura. 1928. Translated by W. H. D. Rouse. Loeb Classical Library. London: William Heinemann.

Philostratus

The Life of Apollonius of Tyana. 1912. Translated by F. C. Conybeare. 2 vols. Loeb Classical Library. London: William Heinemann.

Pliny

Natural History. 1963. With an English translation by W. H. S. Jones. 10 vols. Loeb Classical Library. Cambridge, MA: Harvard University Press, vol. 8: Libri XXVIII–XXXII.

Plutarch

Isis and Osiris: *Plutarch's Moralia in Sixteen Volumes*, Vol. 5. 1936. Translated by F. C. Babbitt. Loeb Classical Library. Cambridge, MA: Harvard University Press.

Fragments: *Plutarch's Moralia in Sixteen Volumes*, Vol. 15. 1969. Translated by F. H. Sandbach. Loeb Classical Library. Cambridge, MA: Harvard University Press.

Suetonius

The Deified Augustus: Suetonius, *Lives of the Caesars, Volume I: Julius. Augustus. Tiberius. Gaius. Caligula.* 1914. Translated by J. C. Rolfe. Introduction by K. R. Bradley. Loeb Classical Library. Cambridge, MA: Harvard University Press.

Tacitus

Germania: *Dialogus, Agricola, Germania.* 1914. Translated by W. Peterson. Loeb Classical Library. London: William Heinemann.

Secondary Literature

Andringa, W. Van. 2007. Religions and the Integration of Cities in the Empire in the Second Century AD: The Creation of a Common Religious Language. In J. Rüpke, ed., *A Companion to Roman Religion.* Oxford: Blackwell, pp. 83–95.

Beard, M. 2004. Writing and Religion. In S. Iles Johnson, ed., *Religions of the Ancient World: A Guide.* Cambridge, MA: Belknap Press of Harvard University Press, pp. 127–38.

Beard, M., J. North, and S. Price. 1998. *Religions of Rome, Vol. I: A History.* Cambridge: Cambridge University Press.

Berchman, R. M. 2007. On Isis and Osiris. In J. Neusner and A. J. Avery-Peck, eds., *Encyclopedia of Religious and Philosophical Writings in Late Antiquity.* Leiden: Brill, pp. 278–9.

Bergman, J. 1968. *Ich bin Isis: Studien zum memphitischen Hintergrund der griechischen Isisaretalogien.* Lund: Almqvist & Wiksell.

Bilde, P. 2013. *The Originality of Jesus: A Critical Discussion and a Comparative Attempt.* Gottingen: Vandenhoeck & Ruprecht.

Blömer, M. and E. Winter, eds. 2012. *Iuppiter Dolichenus, vom Staatskult zur Reichsreligion.* Tubingen: Mohr Siebeck.

Bøgh, B. 2013. The Graeco-Roman Cult of Isis. In L. B. Christensen, O. Hammer, and D. A. Warburton, eds. *Handbook of Religions in Ancient Europe.* London: Acumen, pp. 228–41.

Bremmer, J. N. 2007. Atheism in Antiquity. In M. Martin, ed., *Cambridge Companion to Atheism*. Cambridge: Cambridge University Press, pp. 11–26.

Bricault, L. 2013. *Les cultes isiaques dans le monde gréco-romain*. Paris: Les Belles Lettres.

Burton, P. J. 1996. The Summoning of the Magna Mater to Rome (205 B.C.). *Historia: Zeitschrift für Alte Geschichte* Bd. 45(1): 36–63.

Carobene, G. 2014. Problems on the Legal Status of the Church of Scientology. *Stato, Chiese e pluralismo confessionale* no. 21. June. https://doi.org/10 .13130/1971-8543/4109.

Clauss, M. 2013. The Cult of Mithras. In L. B. Christensen, O. Hammer, and D. A. Warburton, eds., *Handbook of Religions in Ancient Europe*. London: Acumen, pp. 242–62.

Clinton, K. 1992. *Myth and Cult: The Iconography of the Eleusinian Mysteries*. N.p.: Swedish Institute at Athens.

Collins, A. 2014. Alexander's Visit to Siwah: A New Analysis. *Phoenix* 68(1/ 2): 62–77.

Cook, J. G. 2010. *Roman Attitudes towards the Christians: From Claudius to Hadrian*. Tubingen: Mohr Siebeck.

Cotter, W. J. 2010. *The Christ of the Miracle Stories: Portrait through Encounter*. Ada, MI: Baker Academic.

Cowan, D. E. 2023. *The Christian Countercult Movement*. Elements in New Religious Movements. Cambridge: Cambridge University Press. www .cambridge.org/core/elements/abs/christian-countercult-movement/ 60847096CA8D15F8F72D5CF22A03FAF2.

Dalley, S. 2000. *Myths from Mesopotamia: Creation, the Flood, Gilgamesh, and Others*. Oxford: Oxford University Press.

De Ste. Croix, G. E. M. 1963. Why Were the Early Christians Persecuted? *Past & Present* 26 (November): 6–38.

Dillon, M. 2002. *Girls and Women in Classical Greek Religion*. London: Routledge.

Dunand, F. 2007. The Religious System at Alexandria. In D. Ogden, ed., *A Companion to Greek Religion*. Malden, MA: Blackwell, pp. 253–63.

Dzielska, M. 1986. *Apollonius of Tyana in Legend and History*. Rome: L'Erma di Bretschneider.

Ehrman, B. 2014. *How Jesus Became God: The Exaltation of a Jewish Preacher from Galilee*. New York: HarperOne.

Ehrman, B. 2018. *The Triumph of Christianity: How a Forbidden Religion Swept the World*. New York: Simon & Schuster.

Frankfurter, D. 2018. *Christianizing Egypt: Syncretism and Local Worlds in Late Antiquity*. Princeton, NJ: Princeton University Press.

Gallagher, E. 2014. *Reading and Writing Scripture in New Religious Movements: New Bibles and New Revelations*. New York: Palgrave/Macmillan.

Gardner, I. and S. N. C. Lieu, eds. 2004. *Manichaean Texts from the Roman Empire*. Cambridge: Cambridge University Press.

Gnoli, G. 1987. Mani. In M. Eliade, ed., *The Encyclopedia of Religion*, Vol. 9. New York: Macmillan, pp. 158–61.

Gradel, I. 2002. *Emperor Worship and Roman Religion*. Oxford: Clarendon.

Gruen, E. S. 1992. *Culture and National Identity in Republican Rome*. Ithaca, NY: Cornell University Press.

Gruen, E. S. 2016. *The Construct of Identity in Hellenistic Judaism: Essays on Early Jewish Literature and History*. Berlin: De Gruyter.

Hammer, O. 2019. Occult Scriptural Exegesis: Theosophical Readings of the Bible. In B. E. Elness-Hanson and J. Skarpeid, eds., *A Critical Study of Classical Religious Texts in Global Contexts: Challenges of a Changing World*. Pieterlen: Peter Lang, pp. 153–66.

Hammer, O. and M. Rothstein. 2012. Canonical and Extracanonical Texts in New Religions. In O. Hammer and M. Rothstein, eds., *The Cambridge Companion to New Religious Movements*. Cambridge: Cambridge University Press, pp. 113–22.

Hammer, O. and K. Swartz. 2021. Ancient Aliens. In B. E. Zeller, ed., *Handbook of UFO Religions*. Leiden: Brill, pp. 151–77.

Harley-McGowan, K. 2020. The Alexamenos Graffito. In C. Keith, ed., *The Reception of Jesus in the First Three Centuries, vol. 3: From Celsus to the Catacombs: Visual, Liturgical, and Non-Christian Receptions of Jesus in the Second and Third Centuries CE*. London: T&T Clark, pp. 105–40.

Herz, P. 2007. Emperors: Caring for the Empire and Their Successors. In J. Rüpke, ed., *A Companion to Roman Religion*. Malden, MA: Blackwell, pp. 304–16.

Heyob, S. K. 1975. *The Cult of Isis among Women in the Graeco-Roman World*. Leiden: Brill.

Higgins, S. 2012. Divine Mothers: The Influence of Isis on the Virgin Mary in Egyptian Lactans-Iconography. *Journal of the Canadian Society for Coptic Studies* 2–3:71–90.

Hutton, R. 2009. *Blood and Mistletoe: The History of Druids in Britain*. New Haven, CT: Yale University Press.

Kelly, A. and C. Metcalfe, eds. 2021. *Gods and Mortals in Early Greek and Near Eastern Mythology*. New York: Cambridge University Press.

King, K. L. 2003. *What Is Gnosticism?* Cambridge, MA.: Belknap Press of Harvard University Press.

Kyrtatas, D. J. 2010. Historical Aspects of the Formation of the New Testament Canon. In E. Thomassen, ed., *Canon and Canonicity: The Formation and Use of Scripture*. Copenhagen: Museum Tusculanum Press, pp. 29–44.

Lesgourgues, M. 2018. L'écrin sensible de la parole du dieu. Les stratégies sensuelles de mise en condition des acteurs du rite oraculaire dans "l'*Alexandre ou le faux prophète*", de Lucien. *Pallas* 107: 175–96.

Lewis, J. R. and J. Petersen, eds. 2014. *Controversial New Religions*. 2nd ed. New York: Oxford University Press.

Lieu, S. 1992. *Manichaeism in the Later Roman Empire and Medieval China*. 2nd ed. Tübingen: Mohr Siebeck.

Lim, T. 2013. *The Formation of the Jewish Canon*. New Haven, CT: Yale University Press.

MacMullen, R. 2009. *The Second Church: Popular Christianity A.D. 200–400*. Atlanta, GA: Society of Biblical Literature.

Margel, S. 2006. Religio/superstitio: La crise des institutions, de Ciceron à Augustin. *Revue de Théologie et de Philosophie* 138(3): 193–207.

Marjanen, A. 2005. Montanism: Egalitarian Ecstatic "New Prophecy." In A. Marjanen and P. Luomanen, eds., *A Companion to Second-Century Christian "Heretics."* Leiden: Brill, pp. 185–212.

Martin, D. B. 2004. *Inventing Superstition: From the Hippocratics to the Christians*. Cambridge, MA: Harvard University Press.

Martin, L. H. 1983. Why Cecropian Minerva? Hellenistic Religious Syncretism As System. *Numen* 30(2): 131–45.

McGuckin, J. 2008. The Early Cult of Mary and Inter-religious Contexts in the Fifth Century Church. In C. Maunder, ed., *The Origins of the Cult of the Virgin Mary*. London: Burns and Oates, pp. 1–22.

Melton, J. G. 2004. Perspective: Toward a Definition of "New Religion." *Nova Religio* 8(1): 73–87.

Mettinger, T. 2001. *The Riddle of Resurrection: "Dying and Rising" Gods in the Ancient Near East*. Stockholm: Almqvist & Wiksell International.

Metzger, B. 1987. *The Canon of the New Testament: Its Origin, Development and Significance*. Oxford: Clarendon.

Münster, M. 1968. *Untersuchungen zur Göttin Isis: vom Alten Reich bis zum Ende des Neuen Reiches. Mit hieroglyphischem Textanhang*. Berlin: B. Hessling.

Ong, W. J. 1982. *Orality and Literacy: The Technologizing of the Word*. London: Methuen & Company.

Otto, B.-C. 2011. *Magie. Rezeptions- und diskursgeschichtliche Analysen von der Antike bis zur Neuzeit*. Berlin: Walter de Gruyter.

Palmer, S. J. 2009. The Church of Scientology in France: Legal and Activist Counterattacks in the "War on *Sectes.*" In J. R. Lewis, ed., *Scientology.* Oxford: Oxford University Press, pp. 295–322.

Pearson, B. 2007. *Ancient Gnosticism: Traditions and Literature.* Minneapolis, MN: Fortress Press.

Podemann Sørensen, J. 1989. Introduction. In J. Podemann Sørensen, ed., *Rethinking Religion: Studies in the Hellenistic Process.* Copenhagen: Museum Tusculanum, pp. 5–10.

Podemann Sørensen, J. 2011. Hellenismens og den romerske kejsertids religioner. In T. Jensen, M. Rothstein, and J. Podemann Sørensen, eds., *Gyldendals religionshistorie: Ritualer. Mytologi. Ikonografi.* Copenhagen: Gyldendal, pp. 143–70.

Räisänen, H. 2005. Marcion. In A. Marjanen and P. Luomanen, eds., *A Companion to Second-Century Christian "Heretics."* Leiden: Brill, pp. 100–24.

Refslund Christensen, D. 2005. Inventing L. Ron Hubbard: On the Construction and Maintenance of the Hagiographic Mythology of Scientology's Founder. In J. R. Lewis and J. Aagaard Petersen, eds., *Controversial New Religions.* 1st ed. New York: Oxford University Press, pp. 227–58.

Richardson, J. T. 2009. Scientology in Court: A Look at Some Cases from Various Nations. In J. R. Lewis, ed., *Scientology.* Oxford: Oxford University Press, pp. 283–94.

Riley, G. J. 2000. *One Jesus, Many Christs: How Jesus Inspired Not One True Christianity but Many.* Minneapolis, MN: Fortress Press.

Rives, J. B. 1999. The Decree of Decius and the Religion of Empire. *Journal of Roman Studies* 89: 135–54.

Robertson, R. 1991. Globalization, Modernization, and Postmodernization: The Ambiguous Position of Religion. In R. Robertson and W. R. Garrett, eds., *Religion and Global Order.* New York: Paragon House, pp. 281–91.

Roller, L. 1999. *In Search of God the Mother: The Cult of Anatolian Cybele.* Berkeley: University of California Press.

Rose, D. 2019. Ribemont-sur-Ancre, Ritual Practice, and Northern Gallic Sanctuaries from the Third through First Century B.C. PhD dissertation, University of Edinburgh. https://era.ed.ac.uk/handle/1842/36951

Rothstein, M. 2009. "His name was Xenu. He used renegades . . ." Aspects of Scientology's Founding Myth. In J. R. Lewis, ed., *Scientology.* New York: Oxford University Press, pp. 365–88.

Rothstein, M. 2016. Hagiography: A Note on the Narrative Exaltation of Sect Leaders and Heads of New Religions. In J. R. Lewis and I. B. Tøllefsen, eds., *The Oxford Handbook of New Religious Movements.* 2nd ed. New York: Oxford University Press, 392–400.

Rothstein, M. 2017. Space, Place and Religious Hardware. L. Ron Hubbard's Charismatic Authority and the Church of Scientology. In J. Lewis and K. Helleshøi, eds., *Handbook of Scientology*. Brill Handbooks of Contemporary Religion Series, vol. 14. Leiden: Brill, pp. 509–35.

Rothstein, M. In press. Jesus the Sect Leader in Comparative Perspective. *International Journal for the Study of New Religions* 12(1).

Schuhmann, R. 2009. Geographischer Raum und Lebensform der Germanen. Kommentar zu Tacitus' Germania, *c*.1–20. PhD dissertation, Friedrich Schiller University Jena. www.db-thueringen.de/receive/dbt_mods_00013272.

Shaw, B. D. 2015. The Myth of the Neronian Persecution. *Journal of Roman Studies* 105: 73–100.

Shupe, A. and D. G. Bromley, eds. 1994. *Anti-cult Movements in Cross-Cultural Perspective*. New York: Garland.

Smith, J. Z. 1982. Sacred Persistence: Towards A Redescription of Canon. In J. Z. Smith, *Imagining Religion: From Babylon to Jonestown*. Chicago, IL: University of Chicago Press, pp. 36–52.

Stark, R. 1996. *The Rise of Christianity: How the Obscure, Marginal Jesus Movement Became the Dominant Religious Force in the Western World in a Few Centuries*. San Francisco: HarperSanFrancisco.

Takács, S. A. 2008. *Vestal Virgins, Sibyls, and Matrons: Women in Roman Religion*. Austin: University of Texas Press.

Uden, J. 2019. A Crowd of Gods: Atheism and Superstition in Juvenal *Satire* 13. *Classical Philology* 114(1): 100–19.

Van den Broek, R. 2005. Simon Magus. In W. J. Hanegraaff, ed., in collaboration with A. Faivre, R. van den Broek, and J.-P. Brach. *Dictionary of Gnosis and Western Esotericism*. Leiden: Brill, pp. 1069–73.

Vitas, N. G. 2021. *Ex Asia et Syria: Oriental Religions in the Roman Central Balkans*. Oxford: Archaeopress.

Wagemakers, B. 2010. Incest, Infanticide, and Cannibalism: Anti-Christian Imputations in the Roman Empire. *Greece & Rome* 57(2): 337–54.

Wallensten, J. 2014. Dedications to Double Deities: Syncretism or Simply Syntax? *Kernos* 27: 159–76.

Warmind, M. (1999). Om pseudoreligiøsitet. Kriterier for at skelne falske religioner fra sande i antikken og i dag. In P. Bilde and M. Rothstein, eds., *Nye religioner i hellenistisk-romersk tid og i dag*. Aarhus: Aarhus University Press, pp. 53–65.

Weber, M. 1968. *On Charisma and Institution Building*. Chicago, IL: University of Chicago Press.

Weinholt, K. 1989. The Gateways of Judaism: From Simon the Just to Rabbi Akiva. In J. Podemann Sørensen, ed., *Rethinking Religion: Studies in the Hellenistic Process*. Copenhagen: Museum Tusculanum, pp. 87–101.

Williams, M. 1996. *Rethinking Gnosticism: An Argument for Dismantling a Dubious Category.* Princeton, NJ: Princeton University Press.

Wood, S. 1995. Diva Drusilla Panthea and the Sisters of Caligula. *American Journal of Archaeology* 99(3): 457–82.

Worthington, I. 2014. *By the Spear: Philip II, Alexander the Great, and the Rise and Fall of the Macedonian Empire.* Oxford: Oxford University Press.

Cambridge Elements [≡]

New Religious Movements

Founding Editor

†James R. Lewis

Wuhan University

The late James R. Lewis was Professor of Philosophy at Wuhan University, China. He served as the editor or co-editor for four book series, was the general editor for the *Alternative Spirituality and Religion Review,* and the associate editor for the *Journal of Religion and Violence.* His publications include *The Cambridge Companion to Religion and Terrorism* (Cambridge University Press 2017) and *Falun Gong: Spiritual Warfare and Martyrdom* (Cambridge University Press 2018).

Series Editor

Rebecca Moore

San Diego State University

Rebecca Moore is Emerita Professor of Religious Studies at San Diego State University. She has written and edited numerous books and articles on Peoples Temple and the Jonestown tragedy. Publications include *Beyond Brainwashing: Perspectives on Cultic Violence* (Cambridge University Press 2018) and *Peoples Temple and Jonestown in the Twenty-First Century* (Cambridge University Press 2022).

About the Series

Elements in New Religious Movements go beyond cult stereotypes and popular prejudices to present new religions and their adherents in a scholarly and engaging manner. Case studies of individual groups, such as Transcendental Meditation and Scientology, provide in-depth consideration of some of the most well-known, and controversial, groups. Thematic examinations of women, children, science, technology, and other topics focus on specific issues unique to these groups. Historical analyses locate new religions in specific religious, social, political, and cultural contexts. These examinations demonstrate why some groups exist in tension with the wider society and why others live peaceably in the mainstream. The series highlights the differences, as well as the similarities, within this great variety of religious expressions. To discuss contributing to this series please contact Professor Moore, remoore@sdsu.edu.

Cambridge Elements [≡]

New Religious Movements

Elements in the Series

A full series listing is available at: www.cambridge.org/ENRM

Printed in the United States
by Baker & Taylor Publisher Services